FREE
DEVELOPMENTAL TRACKER TEMPLATE
TO USE WITH GUIDE & GROW—BABY'S 1ST YEAR

. . . .

↪ Includes directions and all 3 colors of the developmental trackers for you to save and use each month during Baby's 1st year

↪ Track Baby's accomplishments and milestones, next steps, and memorable moments

↪ Type directly on the tracker of your choice (all are editable) and print

↪ Print the tracker of your choice and write on your hard copy

↪ Use to refer to at appointments with your health care provider

↪ Keep in Baby's book or digital scrapbook

↪ Enjoy looking back at the memories!

Download at:
https://tinyurl.com/devtrackertemplate
or access via QR code:

WHAT OTHERS ARE SAYING.....

"We found this book extremely helpful. As a first-time Mom I wish I would have had this from the beginning! The convenience of having it all in one place is so nice. My sister is currently expecting her first baby and we will 100% recommend her getting this book!"

—Ashley Holland, Mom of 3 month old

"It is a FANTASTIC resource to have for baby's first year! I appreciate that it's more of a guide book, not a thick book with pages and pages of unnecessary words."

—Jordyn Roesler, Mom of 7 month old

"Wish I would've had it when our little one was first born! I thought it was great how you touched on so many different areas and offered ideas for activities...SO useful!

—Michaella Wavra, Mom of 6 month old.

GUIDE&GROW

BABY'S 1ST YEAR

GUIDE&GROW

BABY'S 1ST YEAR

A MONTHLY GUIDE
to Development, Milestones, and
Activities to Support Baby's Development

SHARON DREWLO, OTR/L, CIMI

Sharon Drewlo, OTR/L, CIMI

Book design by G Sharp Design, LLC
www.gsharpmajor.com
"Superbaby" illustration by PremiumClipartShop on ETSY.

ISBN: 978-1-7354862-2-2

"Strengthen a parent, and you strengthen a child."

FRED ROGERS

A MOMENT OF GRATITUDE

I have a heart full of gratitude for the children and families who have welcomed me into their lives and homes over the many years, so we *together* could make a difference in the life of their child. The joy and laughter, the struggles and tears, and celebrating victories both great and small, will forever remain a part of me.

CONTENTS

INTRODUCTION

"I wish I would have known that for my first child."
"Why didn't anyone tell me this?"

...Things I've heard repeatedly in my work with children and families over the past several decades. Many parents are asking for more information to get a thorough picture of their child's development, an understanding of the importance of certain milestones as a foundation for those to follow, and ways to help support baby's developmental skills along the way.

Parents want to be prepared and confident in understanding their baby's development and how to help their little one master developmental skills to reach their greatest potential. I want this too—for EVERY parent, as well as those served through my work as a pediatric occupational therapist, early interventionist, and foster parent.

The amount of information to sift through is often overwhelming for parents and although full of great resources, the online space can be a "noisy" place. When guiding parents in their child's development, I also found myself needing to reference resources in many different places in order to provide a complete picture of a child's development.

Therefore, I created this guide for parents, caregivers and professionals to provide a more thorough look at 9 areas of development and milestones happening in baby's 1st year, as well as activities to promote developmental skills in one easy-to-reference guide.

THIS BOOK PROVIDES YOU WITH:

- A monthly guide to development and milestones in the following 9 areas:

    - Fine Motor

    - Gross Motor

    - Social-Emotional

    - Communication

    - Self-Help

    - Cognitive and Play

    - Visual

    - Visual-Motor

    - Sensory

- Information, activities and strategies to support your baby's development in each month

- Examples of concerns to address with your health care provider and safety tips

- A free PDF developmental tracker template you can download to use to track your baby's developmental achievements each month, use as notes to reference at medical appointments, and keep as a memento in baby's book

- A page for your notes at the end of each chapter

Please note this book is not a medical guide and does not address topics that are of parent choice such as sleep methods, or whether or not to breastfeed for example. Rather, it is intended to be informational and educational in development of the whole child. The developmental information is based on standardized testing, criterion referenced assessments, and evidence based resources, as well as my 31 years of experience and training in working with children and families.

HOW TO USE THIS BOOK

You may choose to check off, highlight, or write dates next to achieved milestones and development. Or you may note baby's achievements on the free PDF developmental tracker template. This can also serve as notes to refer to when at baby's check-ups with your health care provider, print off to keep as a memento in baby's book, or use in an online scrapbook.

This book is not intended to overwhelm you, but instead to provide you with a thorough list of all the amazing developmental achievements your baby can accomplish in the first year! It is important to understand there is a *wide range within typical development* when looking at milestones, with each child developing at a unique and individual rate. Although chapters are organized monthly (except for the first chapter addressing 0-3 months together), you may find your baby has already jumped ahead to the next month with certain skills while catching up on other skills more typical of baby's current month, or even a few skills in the previous month. It is also important to adjust baby's age for prematurity if your little one decided to arrive sooner than expected. If your baby has a known developmental delay or diagnosis, you can still use this book as an informative guide to development for helping baby progress to the next steps at her own pace as you work together with your health care provider and any therapy specialties along the way. Also listed at the end of each chapter are examples of concerns you may want to talk about with your health care provider regarding your baby's development. You know your baby best and there are no silly questions when it comes to your baby's development!

Throughout the book, it is important to remember that information listed regarding sleep and feeding are *average ranges*, again keeping in mind that every baby is unique and develops at an individual rate, and you may be choosing to incorporate certain methods as the parent.

If you are jumping into this book with a 5 month old for example, you may still want to read it from the beginning as there is important information discussed in earlier chapters (such as tummy time, car seats and safety info) that build on or carry over into the following months. Although activities are listed in a specific month, many can overlap and be carried through to the next months, especially if baby enjoys them.

In the activities section to help support your baby's development, examples are given that support the 9 different areas. Keep in mind it is not an all-inclusive list and YOU will come up with many more ideas as you engage, play and get to know your baby. **Being aware of where your baby is in their development and what the next steps are will help guide you best in your play and interactions.** For example, if you know that visually tracking an object to each side is a developmental skill for your baby's age, you may then incorporate this into baby's play, moving objects of visual interest from side to side for baby to follow with her eyes.

As you journey through this first year with your little one(s), I wish you many memorable moments! I hope you find the information shared within this book gives you greater insight into the many miracles and milestones happening before your eyes. Hang on...it's gonna go fast!

Congratulations and a big
"*Welcome to the World*" little one(s)!

DISCLAIMER:

The information and activities in this book are not a replacement for occupational therapy or any other direct therapy services, are not considered medical advice, and should not be used in place of the care of a medical doctor or other qualified healthcare professional. The information is to serve as a guide for developmental skills and activity suggestions to promote development in the first year of life. All activities and recommendations should be facilitated and supervised by an adult with safety as a priority. All activities are to be performed at your own risk, using your judgment, and in no event shall Sharon Drewlo or Forward Therapy Solutions PLLC be liable for any damages. Although information in this book is correct as of press time, recommendations can change overtime, so it is important to check with your healthcare provider and reliable resources such as the American Academy of Pediatrics for updates.

0-3

MONTHS

• • •

BABY'S SUPERPOWER

———

Snuggling and Baby Bonding

FINE MOTOR

- ❑ Hands are primarily closed during the 1ˢᵗ month, then baby begins to open and shut hands more at 2-3 months

- ❑ Grasp reflex is strong when finger is placed in baby's palm

- ❑ Arms typically move together instead of independent of each other

- ❑ When an item such as a rattle is placed in baby's hand, she will hold for up to 30 seconds (2-3 months)

- ❑ Brings one or both hands to mouth (2-3 months)

GROSS MOTOR

- ❑ Will bend and straighten legs when lying on back (alternately or together)

- ❑ Rolls from both right and left sides to back

- ❑ Movement increases with excitement

- ❑ Lifts head to clear nose and turns head during tummy time (1 month)

- ❑ While lying on tummy lifts and holds head and upper trunk 45 degrees bearing weight on forearms or hands (2 months)

- ❑ Arm and leg movements start to get smoother (2 months)

- ❑ When held upright, will bear some weight on legs with knees bent

SOCIAL-EMOTIONAL

- ❑ Interacts with smiling and cooing

- ❑ Calms when held, or to voice and seeing faces

- ❑ Demonstrates increased awareness of others and recognition of familiar faces and objects

- ❑ Startles to loud noises

- ❑ Shows interest with eye contact, but may turn away to indicate she needs a break or is no longer interested

COMMUNICATION

- ❑ Cries differently to communicate needs—when hungry vs tired

- ❑ Makes cooing sounds especially when spoken to; vocal play beginning about 3 months

- ❑ Attends to sounds

- ❑ Discriminates speech from non-speech sounds

- ❑ Prefers "baby talk" and high pitch voices

- ❑ Quiets to parent's voice

SELF-HELP

- ❑ Open and closes mouth in response to stimulation at mouth

- ❑ Uses rhythmic sucking pattern, coordinating suck, swallow and breath pattern from bottle or breast

- ❑ Latches on with a good seal around nipple and tongue moves forward and back to suck during feeding

- ❑ Feeding

Most newborns:

- **Breast-fed:** As baby is hungry or "on demand", about every 1.5-3 hours, gradually nursing less often as they get older.

- **Bottle-fed:** Babies might only take in half ounce per feeding for the first couple days of life, but after that will usually drink 1 to 2 ounces at each feeding. This amount typically increases to 2 to 3 ounces every 3-4 hours by 2 weeks of age.

1 month

- **Breast-fed:** On demand or every 2-3 hours until baby is satisfied

- **Bottle-fed:** 3-4 ounces, 6-8 times/day

2 months

- **Breast-fed:** On demand or every 2-3 hours until baby is satisfied

- **Bottle-fed:** 4-5 ounces, 6-7 times/day

3 months

- **Breast-fed:** Every 2-4 hours until baby is satisfied

- **Bottle-fed:** 4-6 ounces, 6-8 times/day

According to the American Academy of Pediatrics (AAP), a baby should consume, on average, about 2.5 ounces of formula a day for every pound of their body weight. Your health care provider will also be monitoring baby's growth and weight gain.

❑ Baby typically enjoys bath time

❑ Sleeps typically 15-15.5 hours/total

    ▫ 1st and 2nd month: typically 7 hours during the day, split between 3 naps; 8.5 hours at night

    ▫ 3rd month: now closer to 5 hours during the day, still split between 3 naps; may start sleeping through the night about 10 hours at 3 months

COGNITIVE AND PLAY

❑ Enjoys physical contact

❑ Inspects own hands

❑ Looks back and forth between 2 objects

❑ Begins to respond to peek-a-boo (3 months)

VISUAL

1 month

    ❑ Eyes cross at times

    ❑ Likes black and white or high-contrast patterns more than color

    ❑ Enjoys looking at human faces more than anything else

    ❑ Notices stationary objects about 8-12 inches away

- ❑ Newborns especially love black, red, and big squares or polka dots

2 months

- ❑ Focuses visually on objects about 7-8 inches away

- ❑ Becomes active when a toy is seen

- ❑ Responds with a smiling to another smile and looks at faces with interest

- ❑ Vision and eye control are directly related to head position and control—young infants move head and eyes together, with head movements frequently starting first.

3 months

- ❑ Recognizes familiar objects and people at a distance

- ❑ Starts using hands and eyes in coordination together

- ❑ Reacts when your face disappears from view and watches your mouth when you talk face to face

- ❑ Sees objects at a distance of about 12 inches

- ❑ Looks at objects placed in front when held in a sitting position

- ❑ When lying on back, visually tracks an object beyond midline before losing fixation on the object

- ❑ Starts to visually track an object vertically (held about 8 inches away), but may lose focus on the object

The American Optometric Association recommends scheduling your baby's first eye exam around the 6 months of age.

VISUAL-MOTOR

❑ Lying on back, visually tracks an object from midline to each side

❑ Starts to reach toward a seen toy and touch the toy (3 months)

SENSORY

❑ Baby has been listening to sounds since inside the womb. He already recognizes his mother's voice when he is born and responds to new or loud sounds around him with changes in body movement or facial expressions.

❑ Touch is very important starting day one! Baby craves skin to skin contact. Through touch and holding you are teaching your baby that she is loved, safe and secure. You cannot "spoil" a baby by holding her too much. Your baby enjoys firm, surrounding touch that she was used to in the womb. Therefore babies are often comforted by swaddling. She will start to help you learn her favorite ways to be calmed—various movement input such as rocking, swaying or gentle bouncing. She will let you know her favorite positions to be held and often calm to the sound of your voice. By 3 months, your baby may have preferences to touches and textures she finds comfortable, such as a favorite blanket.

❑ Your baby will typically enjoy a variety of movement in different positions by 3 months such as being gently lifted overhead while face to face, or gently tilting baby back in your arms then up toward you while face to face.

❑ Baby can recognize the primary caregiver's scent. This was present at birth but baby has it down to a science now.

. . . .

DID YOU KNOW?

Infants develop more than one million new
neural connections per second!

Most newborns cry without tears until
they are three to six weeks old.

. . . .

WHAT CAN I DO TO HELP SUPPORT MY BABY'S DEVELOPMENT AT THIS AGE?

Remember, YOU are your baby's favorite toy or activity at this age!

When baby is awake and alert, this is your time to engage and get to know each other. Bonding is so important at these early stages. Typical, affectionate touch is important for attachment and early beginnings of engagement and communication. Infant massage is one simple and natural way to incorporate this as a routine to bond with your baby. In addition to the touch and physical benefits, there are many physiological and neurological benefits as well. Infant massage can help with difficulties such as sleep, digestion, and self-regulation. Look for a certified instructor in your area if you want to learn infant massage. It is so much more than "just massage"! Some parents choose to take a class *before* baby arrives so they are prepared to incorporate this into a natural routine starting as soon as day one.

You can't hold your baby too much—they are learning to trust you. When you respond to your baby's crying right away, baby develops a sense of security and they learn that their communication leads to consistency in getting their needs met.

FACE TIME: Definitely not the kind you do on your phone! Actually spending close face-to-face time with your baby while singing, talking, reading, telling stories and showing baby your facial expressions. Babies like to hear higher pitched voices and see better close up at this age. Imitate some of the sounds and noises your baby makes. If your baby is looking at something they are interested in, talk about and describe that object to him. Get excited and show acknowledgment when your baby makes sounds and tries to talk or respond to you. Talk about and narrate what you are doing throughout the day—"We're going to go change your diaper", "Let's go take a bath", or "Look! Daddy's getting the water ready." Baby loves to hear your voice and watch your facial expressions!

Face time.

TUMMY TIME PLAY: The American Academy of Pediatrics' (AAP) updated policy statement and technical report of February 10, 2020, includes new evidence that supports skin-to-skin care for newborn infants; Newborns should be placed skin-to-skin with their mother as soon after birth as possible, at least for the first hour. Infants can especially benefit from skin to skin contact tummy time in the first 2-3 weeks.

Because the American Academy of Pediatrics (AAP) recommends that baby sleeping on his back is the safest position for sleep, it is essential that he spend time on his tummy to learn to move his body against gravity differently than he can when on his back.

Tummy time helps build the strength and skills your baby needs to help meet future milestones. It strengthens the head, neck, and upper body muscles and integrates reflexes that help build the foundations needed for rolling over, crawling, reaching, and playing. It also prevents plagiocephaly (flattening of the head) and positional torticollis (head turned to one side because of tight neck muscles). In addition to these physical benefits, tummy time stimulates brain growth and connectivity; stimulates digestion; encourages eye function for vision, tracking and coordination; and is a wonderful time to be social with baby. Tummy time should start as soon as you bring baby home from the hospital. A great way to begin tummy time with newborns is having baby lie on your chest while you are awake and engaging with him face to face, with you lying back in a reclined position on a chair, bed or the floor.

It is best to do tummy time before feeds and while baby is awake and alert, and always supervised. Recommendations for time on tummy based on age are per the TummyTime!™ Method. It is recommended that babies who are newborn to 2 months of age do tummy time a minimum of 30 minutes per day, split up throughout the day, and supervised during awake times. Start with a few minutes at a time and baby can work up to longer times. By 2-4 months old baby should do tummy time for a minimum of 45-90 minutes per day when awake and alert, again split up throughout the day. Looking ahead to 4-6 months old, aim for 1-2 hours of tummy time per day during awake periods. Once baby is 6-8 months old—the majority of awake time will be on tummy, in sitting and learning to transition to sit.

A blanket on a safe space on the floor is best as it provides a firm, and stable surface for baby to learn to push against. There are different ways to get in baby's tummy time throughout the day other than on the floor and your baby may show his preferences. You can place baby face down supported across your lap. As mentioned previously, baby can lie on your chest or tummy while you are lying back, so that you are face to face. This is great social time with your baby too! When on the floor, get down at eye level with your baby and encourage him to lift his head to make eye contact. You can use a small rolled up blanket or towel for added support under baby's chest, with elbows over and in front of the roll, and elbows aligned under shoulders, but try to use this only if needed for a little support. Avoid making the towel or blanket roll too thick—just enough to support the chest a bit to aid in weight bearing through elbows. This helps avoid hyperextending or over-arching baby's back which can happen if the roll is too thick. You can also try carrying baby using the "football-type hold"—carrying baby tummy down with one hand under the tummy and your forearm between baby's legs, close to your body. Routines to incorporate tummy time may include after drying off from a bath, after diaper changes, during massage or applying lotion, or when getting baby dressed. Some babies do well with tummy time on a large therapy/exercise ball, allowing for gentle movement in different directions and this allows you to adjust how upright baby remains if he is not tolerating being entirely flat on his tummy.

Remember, tummy time can be done in short sessions throughout the day, based on your baby's tolerance and needs. End tummy time if your baby gives you signs he is getting tired such as fussing, crying, or resting face down on the surface.

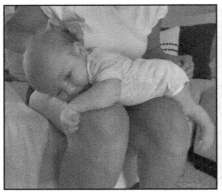

Across the lap.

On your chest or tummy while you are lying back

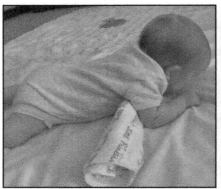

A small rolled-up blanket under chest.

The "football-type hold".

Try to make tummy time fun and stimulating. Join baby face to face on the floor—a great time for storytelling, singing, reading books, or having other objects of interest (toys, baby-safe mirror, musical toy, or water mat) in front of baby. Position objects to baby's right and left to encourage head turning when ready. He especially prefers red, black and white or high-contrast patterns more than color at this age. Move toys and objects to his right and left to encourage head turning and visual tracking. He will be engaged by the colors, pattern, and texture of a blanket or your clothing if lying on you. Many baby toys also have a variety of textures you can help him feel with contact to his palms, in addition to sound stimulation.

There are also baby mat options for tummy time with items of interest attached and with removable U-shaped pillows to assist with propping under baby's chest. These pillows are typically smaller and a much better size than other larger infant safe pillows, which can tend to hyperextend baby's back if used for tummy time, because of their thickness elevating baby's chest. But even these smaller u-shaped pillows still limit baby experiencing weight bearing and weight shift through the elbows. Stop using any small rolls or the small u-shaped pillows under the chest when baby can support herself more on her arms. This will allow her to experience and respond to the weight shift through her arms and remember, *one of the primary goals of tummy time is to develop upper body strength and this will occur best by just having baby on a blanket or mat in a safe spot on the floor, letting baby experience lifting her head up and pushing up against gravity.* You may want to have a tummy time space set up in various areas of your home as a reminder for tummy time when you may be moving about the house with baby. This also varies the sights and sounds of the environment baby gets to experience during tummy time.

Side-lying is another positioning option and it may help to ease baby into tummy time by first spending a little time in side lying before gently helping him roll over to position him on his tummy. When positioning baby on a blanket on his side, you can support his back with your hand or use a small rolled up blanket placed to his back. Make sure both of your baby's arms are in front of him, and slightly bend his hips and knees so your baby is comfortable. As baby grows, he can begin to reach and play from this position.

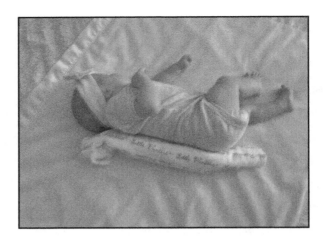

"Side-lying".

If you notice your baby likes to look in a certain direction of interest when placed on the living room floor for example, make sure to change the direction he is lying (or reposition objects of interest) so that he will also turn his head the other direction. Switching sides baby is held in your arms will encourage turning his head to look to both sides. It is also a good idea to alternate which end of the crib or bassinet baby's head is each night, to provide equal opportunity for head turning to both sides, as well as avoiding too much time spent lying on one side of his head which can contribute to flattening of certain areas of baby's head.

It is recommended to limit the time your baby is constrained in baby devices—swings, bouncy seats, car seats, and other baby gear such as exersaucers (aim for no more than a couple hours total time in baby gear each day). *Please see information re: exersaucers in month 6 chapter.* As much as possible, baby needs to freely and actively play on the floor through tummy time as well as on his back and in side lying to help strengthen his muscles and develop foundational skills for later movement. When allowed to move freely on the floor, he will be experiencing frequent success in moving his body against gravity, and in relation to his position, as well as experiencing movement pushing against a solid surface. Although these movements may seem awkward at this stage, each is building on the next to become more and more coordinated. Car seats should be used for travel only, and baby should be removed as soon as you reach your destination, and if sleeping—be placed in a crib or bassinet. This is also recommended if baby falls asleep in other baby gear such as a swing or bouncy seat. Spending too much time in baby gear can hinder developmental skills and prevent correct alignment and use of important muscles in movement. *Also see developmental information and recommendations discussed in Month 6 chapter on exersaucers.*

BACK TIME PLAY: For the times when baby will be on her back and awake, she will love engaging with you—seeing your face, watching your expressions, and hearing your voice. Here are a few other ideas she may enjoy when on her back:

- Mobiles and baby gyms with hanging toys and/or music
- Any visually stimulating toy/book/object or toys that make sound (such as a rattle) moved above baby's face and to each side to encourage head movement, visual tracking, and attending to sound
- Bring different textures/toys to palms for baby to feel and grasp
- Place different textures such as blanket, pillow, stuffed animal, crinkly paper, or even a pan of water at baby's feet for her to kick and feel with her feet.
- There are also baby mats and gyms with a piano for baby to kick when lying on her back.

When your baby is held in different positions, and lies in different positions (tummy, back, side lying), she is also learning through different perspectives and visually orienting to her environment.

In any of your play with baby, also allow for those quiet times of just observing her—watch for baby's cues and expressions. She may look at something attracting her attention, then move her arms and legs in excitement as well as vocalize. Even at this early stage, we can let baby initiate the communication and interaction. Spend some time approaching your baby with only a smile and eye contact, and see how she reacts and initiates the "conversation". She may initiate this with excited movement, a smile, and eyes opening wider, or vocalizing when she sees you. As discussed on the next few pages, these are great opportunities for "serve and return" with your baby as she grows! You will be able to observe baby's cues of readiness for engaging with you when baby is in what's called a "quiet alert state". This state is also an optimal state for feeding and when infants most effectively absorb information.

Signs of this "quiet alert state" are:

- Face is at midline and relaxed

- Any movement of arms and legs are smooth and minimal

- Baby is alert, eyes engaging with you, focused and looking at your face

- Breathing is regular

- Smiling

- Cooing/babbling

When observing, you will also learn your baby's signs and cues of possible "sensory overload". If baby experiences too much stimulation, you may see her disengage by:

- Turning head away

- Breaking eye contact

- Arching back

- Crying, fussing

- Squirming or stiffening arms and legs

- Shutting down and falling asleep

- Frowning

A NOTE ABOUT TOYS AND PLAY:

Although there are many wonderful toys out there, I do not focus on specific toy recommendations. You will find that I mention a few toys and products to reference in order to give you a visual, use as an example, or because it may not be a familiar item. (I am not an affiliate for any of these products). So much of your baby's development happens when you just engage with your baby. YOU are his favorite toy after all! You will find that many of the activity suggestions in each month do not require any specific toy and can involve items of interest to baby that are already in your home or easily accessible. When you know the skill or area of development your baby is working on, there are many options to incorporate toys or items your little one finds of interest; or incorporate many developmental learning activities into baby's daily routines. It's not so much about *what* you're playing with, but more about the *how* you are playing and engaging. In addition to considering age appropriateness and safety, when deciding on toys and activities you may want to ask:

- What are the skills my baby will be working on when playing with this toy or doing an activity? (Keeping in mind a variety of play items and activities that will help promote skills in the various areas of development, as well as being enjoyable and motivating for baby)

- How many different ways can I do this activity or how can this toy be played with beyond what is "on the box"?

- How can I change the environment, my child's position, or the position of the toy to address a different developmental skill?

If I was limited to telling you just *one* thing to keep in mind during play with your baby, it would be to **"play lots of tennis"**. Yep, you read that right—play tennis with your baby. Let me explain...

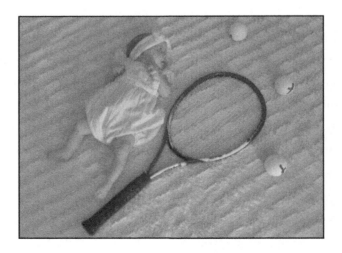

Tennis, anyone?

A big part of tennis is to serve and return. Sometimes you serve, sometimes you return. Neural connections are built and strengthened in a child's brain through these back and forth interactions that are called **"serve and return"**, a term coined by Harvard researchers. Engaging in this responsive turn taking establishes the early beginnings of social-emotional and communication skills needed for a lifetime, promotes bonding, reduces stress responses, and lets baby know she is heard and can trust in responses to get her needs met.

The "serve" may be your baby's cries, a smile, eye contact, vocalizations, facial expressions, movement of arms and legs such as when upset or excited, —all are opportunities for you to establish shared attention, acknowledgment and return the serve. On the "return", you are most likely responding with eye contact, a smile, gestures, picking up baby, giving nurturing touch, meeting a need, and using words to help baby learn about the interaction. In your "return", give baby eye contact and full attention, providing positive and encouraging responses to keep the game going and see how many back and forth interactions you can have before it's "game over". Baby will give you signals when she's overstimulated or done with the interaction. She may divert eye contact or look away, crawl away, or turn her attention to something else of interest. She will also know the game or interaction is over if *you* divert your eye contact, or turn your attention to something or someone else. This is important to keep in mind in the distractions of today, such as when using electronic devices. Babies will know when they've lost your attention or didn't get a "return" to their "serve". Of course life happens and there will be moments when you are unable to respond. But whenever you can, every opportunity to engage in this serve and return is an opportunity to help baby make those connections that impact development and learning.

The wonderful thing is that there are so many opportunities to incorporate this concept throughout baby's day. Here is just one example:

You approach baby lying awake in her crib.

Serve: Baby looks at you and excitedly moves her arms and legs.

Return: "Oh hi baby!" (pause)

Serve: Baby smiles, and moves her arms and legs more.

Return: "You look happy and excited to see me" (pause)

Serve: Baby vocalizes, coos, and smiles.

Return: You may imitate cooing back to baby in addition to using words. (pause)

Serve: Baby responds back to you trying to make the same vocalization

Return: "I love your voice!" (pause)

Serve: Baby looks away and rolls to her side. (cues she is done)

Return (and end): "Ok, we can be all done talking. I think you are ready to get up."

Just this one simple interaction was 5 times "over the net"—5 different engaging and responsive interactions to develop those neural connections in the brain! You will use this game of "serve and return" throughout baby's first year and beyond.

A NOTE ON PACIFIERS:

Sucking is often a baby's first means of self soothing, and many babies have already been sucking on their thumb or fingers in the womb. There are both pros and cons to pacifiers. On the positive side, research has linked pacifiers to reducing the risk of SIDS (Sudden Infant Death Syndrome). It provides a means for baby to calm, and may be easier to wean from than thumb sucking. On the downside, prolonged pacifier use can harm growth and development of oral-facial structures and teeth; can impact speech and language development and affect the development of a mature and safe swallow pattern when moving to more advanced foods.

If breast feeding, the American Academy of Pediatrics (AAP) recommends waiting to offer a pacifier until your baby is 3 to 4 weeks old, and you've established an effective breast feeding routine.

Use pacifiers such as the silicone pacifiers that are all one piece to avoid a choking hazard such as a "2-piece pacifier", and pacifiers should not have ribbons, beads or strings attached. Only give the pacifier if baby is interested. Try to limit pacifier use to naptime or other times baby may need it to help self-soothe by 6 months and try to toss it for good by baby's first birthday.

A NOTE ABOUT SCREEN TIME:

The American Academy of Pediatrics (AAP) recommends children younger than 2 avoid digital media other than video chatting. Media use should be very limited and only when an adult is present or near to co-view and talk, such as when video-chatting with family along with parents. According to the 2016 policy statement—Media and Young Minds by the American Academy of Pediatrics, children under the age of 2 need hands-on exploration and social interaction to develop motor, social-emotional, language and cognitive skills. Evidence suggests that screen viewing before age 18 months has lasting negative effects on children's language development, reading skills, and short term memory and also contributes to problems with sleep and attention.

A NOTE ABOUT CAR SEATS AND GENERAL SAFETY:

www.safekids.org is a great resource to find car seat "inspection stations" and "checkup events" in your area. It is important to know weight and height requirements, when to be forward or rear facing, when to change car seats, and how to make sure they are installed correctly. Safekids.org also has an "Ultimate Car Seat Guide" and area where you can enter your car seat information to see if it has been recalled for any reason.

Throughout each month of this book, safety "pins" (safety tips) are mentioned. For an extensive list of all things "child safety", it is recommended to check out the resources available for you at www.safekids.org or www.cdc.gov. You will find information helpful beyond baby's first year.

If your child has special needs, you may want to consult the National Child Passenger Safety Certification site—through https://cert.safekids.org, where you can search for a certified Child Passenger Safety Technician (CPST) in your area to assist with car seat fitting, positioning, and installation.

- Baby should sleep **alone**, and on her back on a firm surface such as in her crib or bassinet.

- **Only baby** should be in the crib—no blankets, pillows, bumper pads, stuffed toys, or anything soft around baby in her crib or bassinet that may obstruct breathing including sleep positioners.

  An FDA Consumer Update current as of 04/18/2019 states: "The U.S. Food and Drug Administration is reminding parents and caregivers not to put babies in sleep positioners. These products—sometimes also called "nests" or "anti-roll" products—can cause suffocation (a struggle to breathe) that can lead to death." You can find the complete update and a short video at: https://www.fda.gov/consumers/consumer-updates/do-not-use-infant-sleep-positioners-due-risk-suffocation

- Baby should be supervised during tummy time

- If baby starts to roll, it is recommended to stop swaddling

- To minimize forgetting baby in the car, put your purse, briefcase or something you will for sure remember to carry with you in the back seat with baby.

Examples of concerns you may want to talk with your health care provider about—if your baby:

◻ Doesn't seem to respond to loud noises

◻ Doesn't follow moving objects with eyes by 2-3 months

◻ Doesn't smile at sound of your voice by 2 months when you are smiling and talking with your baby

◻ Doesn't cry when hungry or uncomfortable

◻ Doesn't make eye contact or pay attention to faces

◻ Doesn't grasp and hold objects by 3 months

◻ Cannot support head well at 3 months

◻ Keeps head turned to one side most of the time with limitations in turning head fully to the opposite of preferred side

◻ Is developing a flat spot on his head

◻ Is unable to tolerate any tummy time—fusses, cries and/or arches back consistently during tummy time

◻ Has trouble moving one or both eyes in all directions

◻ There is less or weaker movement on one side of the body

◻ Has trouble with turning head to one side more than the other or prefers to keep head to one side

◻ Seems too loose or too stiff in arms, legs or body

◻ Doesn't push down some with legs/feet when held in upright and feet are placed to flat surface (by 3 months)

◻ Frequently resists being held

◻ Is sputtering, coughing, or has any difficulty with coordinating suck-swallow-breathe rhythm for feeding

◻ Is losing a lot of breast milk or formula out the side of mouth during feeding

NOTES

4

MONTHS

. . .

BABY'S SUPERPOWER

—

Can Melt You With a Smile!

FINE MOTOR

- ❑ Grasps a dangling ring or rattle—can sustain grasp while starting to move a rattle

- ❑ Fingers toys, scratches at surface and clutches objects

- ❑ Keeps hands open about 50% of the time

- ❑ Plays with hands at midline while lying on back

- ❑ Brings hands together above chest and hands to hips and knees

- ❑ Brings hands to mouth and object to mouth if in hand

- ❑ Reaches for objects with one hand

- ❑ May start to transfer toys between hands

GROSS MOTOR

- ❑ Lifts head up 90 degrees when on tummy and can hold head steady and centered

- ❑ Pushes up on forearms and brings shoulders off floor— elbows under shoulders or in front of shoulders. Also can turn head to each side while keeping chest off floor.

- ❑ Lifts and turns head to track moving toys or turn to voice/sound

- ❑ When holding baby's hands and gently pulling baby up to sit from lying on back, she should activate her trunk and neck muscles so that there is minimal head lag (head falling back)

- ❑ Rolls from back to sides

- ❑ May start to roll from stomach to back

❑ Pushes down through legs when feet are on a hard surface.

❑ Thrusts legs in play

Pushing up on forearms, shoulders off the floor.

Head up and able to turn head while supporting
self on forearms. Hello there!

SOCIAL-EMOTIONAL

❑ Laughs aloud

❑ Spontaneous social smile—smiles when
seeing you, often before you smile

❑ Anticipates feeding when seeing breast or bottle

❑ Responds to affection

COMMUNICATION

❑ Makes sounds like "ooh" and aah", giggles
and laughs to playful stimulation

❑ Vocalizes in response to hearing own sounds
and when parent repeats baby's sounds

❑ Begins turn-taking behaviors in "conversation" (serve and
return). When there is a pause, baby may vocalize to get you
to talk more, and repeat this back and forth exchange.

❑ Notices difference by demonstrating different reactions to a
happy facial expression and angry or sad facial expression

❑ Begins to notice that tone of voice means different things

SELF-HELP

❑ Sleeps 12-16 hours in 24 hour period; 4-8 hour stretch at night, and usually takes 3 naps, each 1-3 hours long

❑ Places one or both hands to breast or bottle

❑ Watches you eat and may show interest in food

❑ Enjoys bath

❑ Suck-swallow-breathe patterns are consistent and baby has a good suck

❑ Feeding

    · **Breast-fed:** On demand or every 2-3 hours until satisfied.

    · **Bottle-fed:** 4-6 ounces, 6-7 times/day

COGNITIVE AND PLAY

❑ Shows interest in faces and surroundings of environment

❑ Recognizes familiar caregivers and items

❑ Explores and learns about objects primarily with mouth and hand

❑ Hears own sounds and attempts to repeat

VISUAL

- ❏ Eyes follow moving things a few feet away when seated with support

- ❏ Smiles when seeing familiar people

- ❏ Eyes are working better together (binocular vision) to see farther away—about 3 feet

VISUAL-MOTOR

- ❏ Visually targets objects or toys to grasp

- ❏ Hits at dangling objects with hands

- ❏ Looks at object being manipulated in hands

- ❏ When held in supported sitting, will reach for a toy he sees

SENSORY

- ❏ Enjoys a variety of movements

- ❏ Not upset by everyday sounds, and sounds become associated with objects

- ❏ Vision is developing to see up to a few feet

- ❏ Able to calm with rocking, touching and gentle sounds

- ❏ Mouths hands and objects

- ❏ Explores various textures of toys with both hands

- ❏ Most babies at this age are able to link the senses of sight, taste hearing and touch together to form an identity of one object or person

DID YOU KNOW?

There are more sensory receptors in a baby's mouth than anywhere else on his body. Babies learn so much through mouth exploration and it also helps them develop oral motor skills important for eating and talking.

- When baby is rolling, never leave her on the bed, couch or other surface where she may roll off.

- Lots of items are being explored by mouth—make sure only safe items are within reach as she is rolling more.

- If you haven't already, stop swaddling as soon as baby can roll.

What can I do to help support my baby's development at this age?

- Give your baby toys to hold and play with, helping her to feel different textures with her hands, and talk about what she's feeling. In addition to baby toys, look around your home for things that would be safe for baby to hold and feel such as silky scarves or scarves with fringe, plastic measuring cups, a bumpy basket or burlap.

- Baby will learn about cause and effect and sounds when manipulating items that make noise such as crinkly paper, ringing a bell, or shaking a rattle. (Always closely supervise baby when exploring non-baby items.)

- Talk about what your baby is looking at or doing. Narrate what you are doing with baby throughout the day. It's never too early to expose him to many words!

- Tell stories, read books, and sing songs. Make up songs about a picture in a book or a picture of a family member.

▫ Read together—colorful board books or cloth books. Books can be propped up in front of baby during tummy time or held up in front of him when held on your lap. Cloth books may have interesting "taggies", or a corner of a page with different textures to feel and for mouthing, and some cloth books have crinkly paper inside providing sound stimulation.

▫ Baby's mouth is like a 3rd hand to explore and learn about objects! Try to provide items to hold, touch, and mouth that have different textures to explore.

▫ Continue tummy time when awake for a minimum of 45-90 minutes, split up into shorter sessions throughout the day. Place a baby safe mirror, toys of interest, musical toy, or his familiar favorite—YOU—in front of him.

▫ During tummy time, a fun activity to do is put mini flashlights in colored plastic containers, water bottles, or cloth bags. She will be curious about the light so you can roll or move the containers side to side or to and away from her, working on her visual skills. She will also reach for and explore them herself.

▫ Hold toys above your baby at different angles to encourage reaching, or have baby lie under a baby play gym with dangling toys.

▫ Let baby's feet touch different surfaces and talk about them—"this is cold", "this is wet", etc.

▫ Play peek-a-boo, "peeking" from different positions to encourage baby tracking you with his eyes.

▫ Vary your hand placement when holding baby in sitting on a firm surface (gradually moving lower on his trunk as he needs less support) allowing his trunk muscles to get stronger as he learns how to keep his trunk upright when not supported. You may also try a Boppy pillow or other pillows positioned around baby to support him in sitting when he's ready, but always with close supervision. This gives baby a little support but doesn't completely restrict him from moving his trunk to feel and learn how to sit upright. Sitting can be tried for brief periods but baby will still be spending most of his time on tummy, sides and back at this age.

▫ Baby will also like to be held while you walk around, exposing him to different sights and sounds as you talk about them, learning about his world in an upright position.

▫ Allow pauses in conversation to give baby time to process and take her turn to respond and "tell" you something.

▫ Other floor time on back and sides in addition to tummy time—provide a safe space with a blanket on the floor and give baby opportunity to move his body freely and get stronger

Examples of concerns you may want to talk with your health care provider about—if your baby:

▫ Doesn't watch things as they move

▫ Doesn't smile and make eye contact

▫ Doesn't coo or make sounds

▫ Doesn't bring hands or items held to mouth

▫ Has difficulty moving one or both eyes in all directions

▫ Has difficulty with feeding

▫ Has difficulty holding head upright and steady

▫ Has significant difficulty calming even after needs are met and with typical comforting such as holding or rocking

▫ Body seems too stiff or too "floppy"

▫ Keeps head mostly turned to one side or has difficulty turning head to one side

▫ Has a flattened area of head

NOTES

_____

_____

_____

_____

_____

_____

_____

_____

_____

_____

_____

_____

_____

_____

_____

_____

_____

_____

_____

_____

_____

_____

_____

5

MONTHS

• • •

BABY'S SUPERPOWER

—

Using the 3rd hand—the mouth!

FINE MOTOR

- ❑ Holds objects in either hand

- ❑ Holds and shakes a toy or rattle

- ❑ Fingers own hands in play at midline and clasps hands together

- ❑ Transfers a toy from hand to hand, and reaches with both hands

- ❑ Hands are predominantly open

- ❑ Reaches to knees, lower legs, and feet

- ❑ Holds smaller objects with palm and fingers but not yet with thumb

- ❑ Visually controls and orients position of hand prior to grasping an object

GROSS MOTOR

- ❑ Pulls to sit with no head lag. When holding baby's hands and gently pulling her up to sit from lying on back, she should activate her trunk and neck muscles so that her head remains aligned forward and doesn't fall back.

- ❑ Rolls tummy to back and starts rolling back to tummy

- ❑ Sits with assistance and may start to sit unsupported for a few seconds

- ❑ Pushes onto extended arms

- ❑ Starts to pivot on tummy when prone

❑ Sits briefly leaning forward on hands and can rotate head without losing balance

❑ Kicks legs vigorously

❑ Bears almost full weight on extended legs

SOCIAL-EMOTIONAL

❑ Enjoys looking in a mirror and smiles at self in front of a mirror

❑ Responds to affection with a smile

❑ Enjoys playing and can entertain himself for short periods of time

❑ Smiles at and may reach to familiar people

❑ Prefers people over objects

❑ Likes to be sung to

COMMUNICATION

❑ Cries in different ways, including a hunger cry, bored or frustrated cry, and a sleepy cry

❑ Vocalizes more and cries less

❑ Babbles, squeals, and tries to mimic cooing sounds—like "oh" or "ah"

❑ Makes sounds like "goo" and may blow bubbles at the same time

❑ Recognizes different adult facial expressions and will imitate some expressions

❑ Vocalizes when talked to or sung to

❑ (4-6 months) Vocalizes consonant sounds, such as
g and k, and lip sounds such as m, w, p, and b.

SELF-HELP

❑ Sleeps an average of 15 hours every 24 hours, 5 hours
during the day split between 3 naps, and 10 hours at
night if baby has started sleeping through the night

❑ Pats at bottle with both hands

❑ Suck-swallow-breathe patterns are consistent
and baby has a strong suck.

❑ Feeding

- **Breast-fed:** Every 3-4 hours until baby is content or satisfied.

- **Bottle-fed:** 6-7 ounces, 4-5 times/day

❑ Moves head towards spoon with mouth open

- **Solid foods:** 1-3 ounces, 3x/day **IF BABY's READY.** This is
sometimes started between 5-6 months (therefore included
in this month) so it's OK if your baby isn't quite ready yet at 5
months. Many start at 6 months. It is best to check with your
health care provider and important to look for these signs of
readiness:

  □ Baby can hold her head up straight for long periods of
  time when supported upright

  □ Is able to sit upright in a high chair with support and appropriate safety closures

- Shows interest in foods and will lean forward and open mouth for tastes when spoon approaches, and be able to move back or turn head away if disinterested in food

- Baby needs to be able to move food to back of her mouth for swallowing. If she pushes all of the food out of her mouth when trying, then she may not be ready.

- It is noted that the AAP (American Academy of Pediatrics) recommends breastfeeding as the sole source of nutrition for your baby for about 6 months if possible. When you add solid foods to your baby's diet, continued breastfeeding is recommended until at least 12 months. You can continue to breastfeed after 12 months if you and your baby desire. Check with your child's doctor about the recommendations for vitamin D and iron supplements during the first year.

***When introducing a new food, look for signs of a food allergy (rashes, diarrhea, vomiting, irritability, breathing difficulties) while sticking with that food for 3-5 days before introducing a different new food. You may also want to ask your pediatrician for any recommended medications to have on hand in case baby does have an allergic reaction, or other medication needs such as in the case of a fever. For more information on allergies visit www.foodallergy.org*

Volume is NOT the initial goal of introducing baby food. Initially, it is best for baby to explore, get messy, play with and learn about foods. You may want to put a plastic mat or table cloth under the chair, dress in old clothes or just have baby in a diaper if the room is warm enough. Place some of the baby food on the tray and let her explore with her hands and get messy. This is important sensory exploration that is telling her about the textures, smells and looks of food so she can get as much information as possible about the food before it goes into her mouth. Once food is in the mouth baby can no longer see it or feel it with her hands, and the only sensory system giving baby information about the food is her oral sense and sometimes her sense of smell depending on the food. This early exposure and exploration with foods can be key to less "picky" eating later on.

Avoid cleaning baby's face with a cloth or scraping with the spoon after bites, as baby may have aversion to constantly being cleaned and therefore this may create a negative response associated with feeding. It is recommended to save clean up until after the feeding is completed. You may also try to clean up baby at the kitchen or bathroom sink, so that she will associate the feeding as a positive experience especially if she doesn't like her face wiped clean.

After about 2 weeks of first trying plain baby food cereal, offer a baby food puree mixed in with the baby cereal. Remember to only introduce one new food every 3-5 days to make sure there is no food allergy. An example would be to alternate a fruit with a vegetable every 3 days.

It's great to let baby observe food preparation in the kitchen, be near the smells, and be a part of your family meals even if just observing.

COGNITIVE AND PLAY

❑ Learning cause and effect and how to get a reaction

❑ May understand object permanence (4-7 months)—
meaning that objects don't permanently disappear
when they are out of sight. Therefore baby may
start to cry when seeing you leave the room.

VISUAL

- ❑ Turns head while lying on back to look for a dropped object

- ❑ Eye movements are more disassociated from head movement

- ❑ Looks from one object to another of 2 objects within view

- ❑ Stares at a rattle placed in his/her hand

- ❑ When in a supported sitting position, turns head past midline to watch a large ball slowly rolled by from one side to the other

- ❑ Looks at a small object (about the size of a raisin) a foot or 2 away and will reach for it

- ❑ Eye rods and cones develop at 5 months allowing baby to begin seeing in color

VISUAL-MOTOR

- ❑ Looks at and reaches for a toy with both hands

- ❑ Looks at object he/she is holding

SENSORY

- ❑ Enjoys a variety of movements

- ❑ Not upset by everyday sounds, and sounds become associated with objects

- ❑ Able to calm with rocking, touching, music and gentle sounds

- ❑ Mouths hands and objects

- ❑ Explores toys both orally and visually the most, but is starting to explore more with hands

. . . .

DID YOU KNOW?

Your baby is already experiencing a whole range of feelings like joy, sadness, anger, interest and excitement.

. . . .

SAFETY "PINS"

- Never leave small objects in your baby's reach, as baby most likely will put them in his mouth.

- Baby will be grabbing at many things so keep all hot liquids such as your coffee cup out of reach to prevent burns, and sharps or anything else harmful to baby, out of reach.

What can I do to help support my baby's development at this age?

- Continue all that good tummy time—a minimum of 1-2 hours split up throughout baby's awake times. Space favorite items not only in front, but to right and left sides of baby to encourage reach, weight shift on arms, and baby may start to pivot on tummy to get to desired items.

- Start a band! (supported sitting or high chair if needed) Give baby a few items such as wooden spoons and some pots or pans to bang on, or small maracas, and bell rattles. You can place a few beans in a small plastic bottle with a secure lid for a homemade shaker. Baby may also enjoy banging at a toy piano or other sound making toy.

- Read books with colorful pictures and shapes, and talk about the pictures. Baby will love to look at pictures of himself and other familiar family members. Name people in the pictures and tell baby all about them!

- Continue to talk to baby and narrate throughout your day. Respond to her vocalizing and "talking" as if you understand what she is communicating.

- When playing, hold up 2 items and ask baby which one she wants to play with. She may "tell you" by gazing longer at her choice or reaching toward her choice.

- Peek-a-boo with you and show baby peek-a-boo with herself in front of a mirror. Have baby pull a cloth off of her head or your head.

- Baby is now seeing color, so talk about and expose her to colors in books, brightly colored toys, or other colorful objects in different environments.

- Help baby touch and experience different textures outdoors—snow, tree bark, grass, leaves, or flowers, and smell safe items.

- She may enjoy sensory bags (example pictured below) especially during tummy time or when in her highchair. These are easy to make and there a lot of options on Pinterest or other sites. Example: Place hair gel, water, or a clear-like shampoo inside a large Ziploc bag (gallon size). Add glitter, water beads, marbles, other various beads, little plastic fish or other small colorful items of interest that won't poke through. Securely tape the bag on all sides and corners to avoid any leaking. This should be always supervised for any opening or leaking of the bag. Baby will enjoy trying to grab the items, look at the colors and various items, and will be able to feel how things squish and move. You can also place a few drops of paint on paper then slide the paper into a clear plastic bag, seal and tape edges to secure, and let baby work on her masterpiece!

Sensory Bag painting.

Sensory Bag with colorful and shiny objects.

- Help baby sit on your lap or the floor with only the amount of support needed to keep her safe so that she can use her muscles to get stronger for sitting and help her body learn how to respond to changes for balance and keeping upright. To start she may need your hands holding her further up on her ribcage, and as she gets stronger, only need to have your hands at her hips as she controls her trunk.

- Hold and moving baby safely through the air provides input to her vestibular system—move up and down (gently lifting overhead), bounce on your knee, move side to side or in a circle, while safely and securely held.

- Provide a variety of different textured baby safe items for mouthing and teething. Never leave a baby unattended with a teething item. Look for ones with different textures and shapes. Teethers or mouthing toys that get back onto the molar area allow baby to strengthen biting and get some relief beyond just the front of his mouth. Examples are: ZoLi Bunny Dual Nub Teether (https://zoli-inc.com/products/bunny-7), Baby Teething Tubes (https://babyteethingtubes.com/), and The Molar Magician recommended to use without the Companion Clip for safety reasons (https://tinyurl.com/y5g7n8sp).

- Baby will enjoy toys and items she can hold well, pass between her hands and bring to her mouth

- She may enjoy foot rattles or fun socks encouraging reaching to her feet (typically between 5-8 months) or tie the string of a helium balloon around baby's ankle (always supervised) to encourage her kicking and watching it move, floating a few feet above her.

- If you happen to have a hulahoop, you can wrap and affix different material/textures at intervals around the hulahoop. Place baby in the middle of the hula hoop on her tummy on the floor, to encourage pivoting around on her tummy to explore the different textures (try ribbons, tinsel, socks, netting, scarves). Of course as with any play mentioned, baby should be supervised especially if everything is going to the mouth!

Hula Hoop with materials/textures attached

Examples of concerns you may want to talk with your health care provider about—if your baby:

- Crosses eyes frequently or eyes are out of alignment
- Doesn't watch items or people as they move
- Is unable to hold head up and steady
- Is not able to sit up at all with support
- Doesn't bring hands or other items to mouth
- Does not seem to respond to or is uninterested in your face
- Isn't smiling
- Doesn't grasp or manipulate toys or objects
- Doesn't coo or vocalize
- Doesn't respond to sounds
- Cries or fusses during all tummy time
- Has difficulty with sleep
- Has difficulty with feedings
- Makes no attempts to roll
- Doesn't bear any weight on legs when feet are placed to floor or surface
- Has stiff or awkward movements, or seems too "floppy"

NOTES

_____

_____

_____

_____

_____

_____

_____

_____

_____

_____

_____

_____

_____

_____

_____

_____

_____

_____

_____

_____

_____

_____

_____

_____

_____

6

MONTHS

• • •

BABY'S SUPERPOWER

——

Super Sensory Detective

FINE MOTOR

- ❑ Retains grasp of a rattle when shaking

- ❑ Reaches and uses a raking type grasp to obtain objects

- ❑ Holds a small object with palm, fingers and thumb

- ❑ Releases grasp to drop an object from each hand

- ❑ Keeps hands open rather than in fists, at least half of the time

- ❑ Passes objects from hand to hand

- ❑ Demonstrates a controlled reach—can stop and start reaching movement at different points in the range

GROSS MOTOR

- ❑ Head is erect and steady when sitting— fully developed head control

- ❑ "Ring" sits (as pictured) briefly with hands free to manipulate a toy or object

Ring sitting with hands free.

❑ Pivots in circle while lying on tummy

❑ Begins to push up into a crawling position (falling forward initially) and may do some rocking back and forth on hands and knees

❑ Takes full weight on legs in supported standing

❑ Will do consecutive rolls across the floor to get to something

SOCIAL-EMOTIONAL

❑ Enjoys social play and playing with others

❑ Vocalizes pleasure and displeasure with different sounds

❑ Lifts arms toward parent

❑ Can discriminate strangers

❑ Laughs and smiles

❑ Listens and responds when spoken to

❑ Responds to angry voice with a frown

❑ Likes to look at self in a mirror

COMMUNICATION

❑ Turns head to localize sound and voice

❑ Happily experiments making different sounds— grunting or growling, babbling

❑ Has longer duration of sounds

❑ Vocalizes to sound stimulation or speech

❑ Responds to pauses in conversation with taking his turn to "talk" with sounds/babbling

❑ Looks and vocalizes to own name

❑ Vocalizes to get attention and express feelings

❑ Uses consonant sounds in babbling, e.g. "da", and "ba", and "ga" sounds

SELF-HELP

❑ Places both hands on a bottle or breast

❑ Strong suck with no loss of liquid

❑ Feeding

- **Breast-fed:** Every 3-4 hours until baby is content or satisfied.

- **Bottle-fed:** 6-8 ounces, 4-5 times/day

- **Solid food:** 1-3 ounces 3 times/day **IF BABY'S READY (see signs of readiness and feeding information in 5 months chapter)**

  □ 6 months—Thin baby food cereals

  □ 6 ½ months—Stage 1 thin baby food purees with slightly thicker baby food cereals

Talk with your pediatrician about the current guidelines on when to introduce allergenic foods such as milk, egg, soy, wheat, peanut, tree nuts, fish, and shellfish.

***When introducing a new food, look for signs of a food allergy (rashes, diarrhea, vomiting, irritability, breathing difficulties) while sticking with that food for 3-5 days before introducing a different new food. You may also want to ask your pediatrician *for any recommended medications to have on hand in case baby does have an allergic reaction, or other medication needs such as in the case of a fever. For more information on allergies visit www.foodallergy.org*

❑ Uses some up and down chewing movements

❑ Starts to eat small amounts of thin, pureed foods such as infant cereal or pureed fruit from a spoon

❑ Opens mouth to presentation of spoon and actively lowers upper lip to spoon.

   ▫ With spoon at baby's mouth, pause and allow her to try to re-move the food from the spoon with her lips as much as pos-sible,—avoid "scraping" the food off when you remove the spoon from her mouth. This will help her work on lip move-ment and closure to remove food from the spoon.

❑ Sleeps an average of 14.5 hours every 24 hours, 3.5 hours during the day split between 2 naps, 11 hours at night

❑ You may have already been massaging baby's gums to soothe teething. If baby has teeth, it is recommended to start brushing them. You can use a damp gauze pad, tooth wipe or finger brush made for infants to start cleaning baby's teeth, using only a rice-grain-size amount of *fluoride containing toothpaste.* Making sure baby doesn't fall asleep with a bottle in her mouth will help keep teeth healthy too. *Plan to see a dentist when baby turns 1.*

❑ Babies at 6 months typically have the basic oral motor skills to begin to experiment and learn how to drink from an open cup with your help. You can practice this with small sips between **6-9 months if baby is sitting upright independently with good head control, and holding objects well.** Cups like the Flexi Cut Nosey Cup (https://www.amazon.com/Flexi-Cut-Cup-Pink-Pack/dp/

B0056PPGOY) or the Ezpz tiny cup (https://ezpzfun.com/products/tiny-cup?variant=19432577826885) can help this transition. Let baby play with and feel the empty cup to explore it first. Make sure she is sitting upright well in her highchair. You will hold the cup while offering a small amount of baby's favorite puree in the cup, and then small sips of breast milk or formula. The cup should be full enough so that baby doesn't have to tilt her head far back. It's ok if she wants to grab the cup and bring to her mouth—just guide her so that you control the flow of liquid. If she has a lot of coughing or choking even on small sips she is probably not ready. Babies also can transition with recessed lid cups such as The Munchkin Miracle 360 Trainer (https://tinyurl.com/yxbzstqx). The cup automatically seals when baby stops drinking so it eliminates spills, while allowing drinking from anywhere around the rim—just like a regular cup. When baby drinks, it activates the flow of liquid and helps support normal muscle development in baby's mouth.

Sometimes as soon as 6 months and more often closer to 8-9 months, baby can also start learning to drink from a straw. Therefore I am including this information here, but remember—follow baby's readiness cues, and there is plenty of time for practice. Occupational Therapists and Speech Therapists who specialize in feeding, recommend skipping sippy cups when possible and sticking with a straw cup or open cup. Using a sippy cup spout is similar to sucking on a bottle, and exclusively using sippy cups can limit your little one in developing a mature swallow pattern, and affect tongue position in the mouth for speech patterns. There are now several choices of straw cups available with flexible straws once baby masters straw drinking, such as this ZoLi Straw Cup (https://tinyurl.

com/yy8jp79b) or the Munchkin Straw Trainer Cup (https://tinyurl.com/y2zgs628).

Therapists trained in feeding skills often use "honey bear straw cups" to teach straw drinking (https://www.amazon.com/Talk-tools-Honey-Drinking-Flexible-Straws/dp/B013RAKUQS). They are just like the honey bear containers you may be picturing from the grocery store, but without the honey, and have a flexible straw through the top. They allow for liquid to be squeezed up the straw in a controlled manner to help baby initiate sucking on the straw.

Trying the Honey Bear Straw Cup.

Another option are the First Years Take & Toss Straw Cups. (https://www.amazon.com/First-Years-Spill-Proof-Straw/dp/B0054YZDWC). (They are actually reusable so you really don't have to toss them as the name implies.) They also allow for you to squeeze the cup a bit to help the liquid get up the straw (but the straws are *not* flexible). It doesn't take much squeezing—experiment over a sink first and practice squeezing so that only a tiny amount reaches baby's mouth. The straw fits in the hole snuggly so if it tips over there is usually only minimal spilling (depending on baby's throwing abilities!)

It is recommended to practice open cup drinking before straw drinking, but do continue to offer both. Because baby may be able to suck purees from her spoon, she may also naturally suck when a straw is placed to her mouth. But she is not used to sucking something up the length of a straw. It is best to start with a thin puree that can be sucked through a straw. You can teach your baby by putting the straw in the puree, then place your finger over the top of the other end to hold a small amount of puree in the straw.

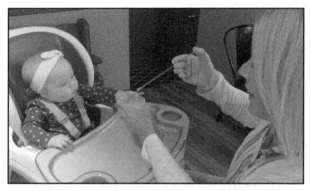

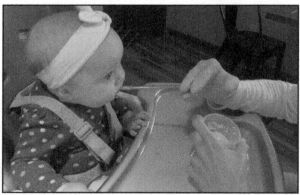

Straw teaching technique.

While baby is sitting upright in her highchair, place the straw to her mouth (slightly above horizontal) and when you release your finger let a small amount of puree flow into her mouth. Baby should close her lips around the straw and may start to suck. Gradually work toward baby sucking out the puree instead of you having to release it into her mouth. Once she gets the hang of it you can try moving the straw directly into a cup, helping her to control the amount she sucks up to coordinate with the swallow. Once she is coordinating sucking thin puree up through the straw and swallowing without difficulty, you can then try breast milk or formula. **Remember you can work on this over time starting 6-9 months, if baby's ready. Some babies may not be ready to try straw drinking until closer to 9 months.** Check with your health care provider about the recommended amount of water baby can have for her age when starting to work with sips from an open cup.

COGNITIVE AND PLAY

❑ Intentionally drops an object to watch it fall

❑ Demonstrates curiosity about things and tries to get things out of reach

❑ Figures out how to get other's attention making all kinds of sounds other than crying

VISUAL

❑ Tries to get a dropped toy if she can see it while lying on her back

❑ Has full color vision

❑ Can focus on objects near and across a room

❑ Depth perception is improving

❑ Examines objects more closely

❑ When lying on back, eyes follow an object moved side to side at about an 8 inch distance

The American Optometric Association recommends scheduling your baby's first eye exam around the 6 months of age.

VISUAL-MOTOR

❑ Grabs own foot or feet when lying on back

❑ Visually targets, reaches for and touches a tiny piece of food

❑ Bangs small objects on table

❑ If bottle fed, can get bottle to mouth by self

SENSORY

❑ Localizes tactile stimulation by touching the same spot that was just touched by someone, or searches for object that touched body

❑ Uses both hands to explore the feel of toys and other items such as a blanket or clothing

❑ Experiments with the amount of force needed to pick up different objects

❑ Continues to explore with mouth

❑ Enjoys a variety of movements in play—in your arms and also through movement play on the floor

❑ Calms to parents voice, singing, and/or to rocking and holding

· ·

DID YOU KNOW?

Having music or television on in the background can make it harder for babies to distinguish the voices around them and pick up language. Babies love music but it is best as a focused activity, not background noise.

· ·

SAFETY "PINS"

- In preparation for baby becoming more mobile and crawling (maybe he already is!) in the months to come, find those hidden dangers before your baby does. The best way to do this is get down on your hands and knees at "baby level" and look around for both obvious and hidden dangers that baby may discover.

- AAP (American Academy of Pediatrics) News posted the following FDA warning of December 20, 2018: "Children should not use teething jewelry, which can lead to choking or strangulation, according to a warning from the Food and Drug Administration (FDA). They also recommend to "Avoid gels, creams and other products containing benzocaine, which can lead to a life-threatening reduction in oxygen carried by the blood". For information on the complete FDA warning, visit https://tinyurl.com/y3rdl3lo.

What can I do to help support my baby's development at this age?

- Try not to overwhelm baby with a lot of toys around him. At times you may choose to present him with just one toy to let him focus and explore. Other times you may have several placed around him to choose.

- Have a small basket or container with a few items in it for baby to work on getting the items out.

- Continue to provide a variety of teethers and other safe items for baby to explore with his mouth, as mentioned in month 5 chapter.

- Hold up 2 toys/items or 2 books for baby to choose which one he wants. He may choose by reaching for it or just looking at one for a longer period to let you know.

- At Laundry Time: Touch and feel the different textures of clothing items. Play peek-a-boo or playfully hide a toy under a towel.

- Time in the Kitchen:

    - Let baby watch, hear, smell all that is going on in the kitchen

    - Let him feel and explore safe food items (orange, squash, apple) and watch how a food changes such as in the process of peeling an orange or peeling a banana then cutting into pieces. This is all important exposure to food for baby!

    - Yogurt painting: yogurt mixed with natural food colorings on high chair tray. Pudding and whipped cream work too. (be mindful of allergies and ingredients when first exposing baby)

    - Explore other baby food purees on his tray for messy play and exposure to textures, smells, and tastes if he happens to bring hands to mouth

    - Make colored ice cubes using food coloring and have baby explore on a cookie tray or on high chair tray

    - Give your baby safe kitchen items to bang, manipulate, mouth and explore—plastic measuring cups, silicone spatula, wooden spoon, lids and bowls.

- Outside play: Talk about and name things you are seeing, smelling, hearing, and feeling outside. Take tummy time outside on a blanket and let him feel the grass.

- Continued tummy time is important! Baby should spend a minimum of 1-2 hours on tummy each day when awake. As baby starts to move more, lay out a "blanket" of various textures on the floor to explore during tummy time such as a rug, towel, rubber bath mat, silky sheet, and a fuzzy blanket.

▫ Lots of reading, singing and story-telling! Remember to pause and let your baby initiate getting your attention and telling you a few things too.

▫ Continue to talk about everything you are doing with baby, naming and talking about things throughout the day and in different environments.

▫ Show him pictures of family members and pets, name them and talk about them. You may want to put pictures in a baby safe photo book for him to explore.

▫ Bubbles—so fun to watch and good for visual tracking. Catch one on the bubble blower ring and hold it out for baby to pop. Say "pop!", and see if she notices the wet feeling. Of course watch for soapy hands going to her mouth!

▫ Dance! Baby will love your fun moves and bouncing, twirling, or swaying in your arms while having fun and experiencing lots of good movement input.

▫ Music toys, clapping, shaker sound toys, making funny sounds with your mouth, or try whistling or humming for baby

▫ Glitter bottles/sensory bottles, sensory bags

  ▫ Glitter, sequins, and other small objects in a plastic bottle with secured lid—either in water (you may choose to col- or the water) or without. There are many variations online.

  ▫ Sensory bags as described in month 5. You don't have to use hair gel in the plastic bags. Try some without the gel and just put the items in the bag—it will be different to feel and manipulate, and some items may make sound when manipulated. Search sensory bags for infants online and you will find many options.

  ▫ You can also put paint drops on a piece of paper, then place it in a plastic bag and seal. Watch baby turn it into their very first "painting" either during tummy time or sitting in high chair as pictured in photo on p. 53.

▫ Mirror play—smile, make faces and funny sounds in the mirror, pat at and feel mirror

▫ Bath time: Baby will have fun splashing, kicking, and when supported in sitting he will be figuring out how to grasp toys when they are wet or floating away. Name body parts as you are washing or make up a song about washing and bath time.

▫ Dressing: When dressing or undressing baby, playfully talk about body parts and what you are doing—"arm goes in", "socks go over toes", or "where is baby?" when a shirt goes on/off over his head.

▫ When baby runs errands with you, he is getting exposed to different environments with different sights, sounds and smells that you can tell him about.

▫ Supervised play exploring rope lighting of different colors

▫ Place items out of reach to encourage problem solving to move toward them.

▫ Baby might not yet be able to do the actions but will love to see YOU do the actions to songs such as "Itsy Bitsy Spider"

▫ Cut gelatin in blocks to explore on a tray for sensory play

▫ Scarves or handkerchiefs for baby to pull out of things like shape sorter holes, a paper towel core tube, or empty Kleenex or wipes box.

▫ Spend some time doing nothing—just being with, observing and enjoying baby, allowing him to initiate his play or interactions.

▫ Pediatric Occupational and Physical therapists typically recommend limiting time in exersaucers (as well as any bouncer or jumper) to 15-20 minutes a day, due to poor posturing and poor standing position with fabric between legs pulling hips apart; encouraging baby to lock out his knees and be up on his toes instead of bearing weight over the whole foot. Babies who spend a lot of time in exersaucers are in a position where their center of gravity remains forward, and they also cannot see their feet to get the visual input when learning to stand and balance. When babies are developing balance in standing, their muscles and joints send messages to the brain when there is a loss of balance so that they can learn and experience correcting their position in order not to fall. This doesn't happen when in the exersaucer because they are supported and can lean on the edges. This forward position takes weight off of the hips and gluteal muscles which are actually the ones that need to be strengthened for crawling and standing, along with pelvic and core musculature. Exersaucers also limit active exploration of baby's environment, which develop cognitive and motor skills—through rolling, crawling, scooting—allowing baby to actively figure out how to get to and manipulate items that are not just stationary or fixed (like the ones fixed on the exersaucer ring). Some exersaucers say they can be used with infants as young as 4 months, but it is recommended that baby be able to sit independently with arms free to minimize moving into the poor posturing mentioned above. If you are going to use an exersaucer, it is best to wait until 6-7 months, and try to limit to 15-20 minutes a day. Check baby's foot position—you may need to place a pillow under his feet so that he is not up on his toes, toes curled under, totally flat footed, or ankles rolled onto sides.

Poor posturing in exersaucer.

Examples of concerns you may want to talk with your health care provider about,—if your baby:

- Doesn't smile or show affection for parents or caregivers
- Doesn't respond to sounds, only responds to certain sounds (loud or certain pitch, or only seems to notice sounds from one side or ear)
- Has difficulty with eating or drinking
- Isn't vocalizing vowel sounds and babbling
- Doesn't laugh out loud
- Seems very stiff or very "floppy" in limbs, head/neck, and/or trunk
- Doesn't roll over in either direction
- Doesn't try to get things that are in reach
- Misses items when reaching for them, appearing not to see them well
- Doesn't seem curious about exploring toys
- Uses one side of the body significantly less than the other
- Doesn't bear much weight on legs when held in standing position with feet on surface or floor
- Demonstrates one or both eyes drifting or not working together well

NOTES

7

MONTHS

• • •

BABY'S SUPERPOWER

———

No Hands Super Sitter

FINE MOTOR

- ❏ Passes objects between hands

- ❏ Uses a raking grasp and can get small objects into palm

- ❏ Retains toy in one hand while reaching for another toy with opposite hand

- ❏ Pokes or examines objects with index finger

- ❏ Reaches for objects with one hand instead of two

- ❏ Bangs objects on a table, tray, floor

- ❏ Turns objects in different ways to examine and explore

GROSS MOTOR

- ❏ Lifts head when lying on back as if to get up

- ❏ Raises hips off the ground while pushing with feet (while lying on back)

- ❏ Sits erect and unsupported for about five minutes

- ❏ Can maintain sitting balance while using arms/ hands to hold and manipulate a small toy

- ❏ Pivots around on tummy during play

- ❏ Pulls self along the floor, dragging body or in low creeping position

- ❏ Gets onto hands and knees and rocks back and forth

- ❏ Can move from hands and knees into sitting

- ❏ Bounces actively when supported in standing

SOCIAL-EMOTIONAL

❑ May laugh at peek-a-boo and enjoys getting a reaction

❑ Works for a toy which is out of reach

❑ Likes to explore adult faces and hair

❑ Understands what to do to get your attention

❑ Can discern a voice's emotional state

COMMUNICATION

❑ Jabbers with vowel sound combinations (*eh, ah, oh*)

❑ Begins to use repeated syllables over and over (6-9 months) such as "bababa, dadada, mamama"

❑ Understands and responds to name

❑ Turns to listen to familiar sounds such as a phone ringing

❑ Shakes head "no"

❑ "Talks" (babbling) to a toy or pet of interest

❑ Looks and vocalizes to own name

❑ Babbles to others and may try to copy your voice tone and patterns

❑ May start to demonstrate understanding of short phrases such as showing excitement to "let's go" or "bath time"

❑ Looks toward family member when named, such as looking toward Daddy when you say "Where's Daddy?"

SELF-HELP

- ❑ Holds and tips bottle to drink independently

- ❑ May gag on new puree textures

- ❑ Has more movement of tongue up and down
  and to the side when chewing food.

- ❑ Brings lower lip to spoon; moves upper lip forward,
  down, and then inward to remove food from spoon.

- ❑ When holding spoon to mouth, allow baby to try to remove the food
  from the spoon with her lips as much as possible,—avoid "scraping"
  the food off when you remove the spoon from her mouth. This
  will help her work on lip closure on the spoon to remove food.

- ❑ Feeding
  - · **Breast-fed:** Every 3-4 hours until baby is content or satisfied.
  - · **Bottle-fed:** 6-8 ounces, 4-5 times/day
  - · **Solid food:** 4-6 ounces 3 times/day (Stage 1 type—thin baby
    food purees)

  ***When introducing a new food, look for signs of a food allergy (rashes, diarrhea,
  vomiting, irritability, breathing difficulties) while sticking with that food for 3-5 days
  before introducing a different new food. You may also want to ask your pediatrician
  for any recommended medications to have on hand in case baby does have an
  allergic reaction, or other medication needs such as in the case of a fever. For more
  information on allergies visit www.foodallergy.org*

- ❑ **See cup and straw drinking information in Month 6 chapter**

- ❑ Sleeps about 11 hours at night (many straight through) and
  naps 3-4 hours during the day split between 2 naps

- ❑ Usually tolerates diaper changes without crying

- ❑ Enjoys bath and playing in the water

COGNITIVE AND PLAY

❑ Takes items out of containers

❑ Understands how objects can be used to get a sound or reaction

❑ Searches briefly for an object when it's taken away

❑ Problem solves by adjusting own position to get a toy out of reach

❑ Finds a partially hidden object

❑ Beginning to learn about heights, distance, and space

VISUAL

❑ Eyes track an object 180 degrees from side to side while sitting

❑ Eyes follow a falling object to the floor when dropped

❑ Visually targets an object that is out of reach and tries to get it

❑ Demonstrates depth perception

VISUAL-MOTOR

❑ Reaches for small objects with just one hand

❑ Starts to coordinate eyes and hands for clapping

❑ Visual information is guiding baby's actions more—
how to manipulate an object or how to act on an
object to get movement or a sound for example

❑ Will reach for and touch image of self in mirror

SENSORY

- ❑ Able to hear and pick up on the specific parts of speech and the way words form sentences

- ❑ Not fearful of everyday sounds in typical environments

- ❑ Calms to rocking, touch, cuddling, soothing, or parent's voice

- ❑ Naturally prefers sweet tastes and may need multiple presentations of the same food to taste before deciding he/she likes it or not

- ❑ Shows strong reactions to new smells and tastes

- ❑ Enjoys exploring different textures of toys, blankets, carpet, clothing and touch-and-feel books

- ❑ Continues to mouth objects for exploration and teething

- ❑ Enjoys affection—touches, kisses, snuggling

- ❑ Observes and orients to environment from different positions—lying on tummy or back, sitting, hands and knees, and supported in standing

- ❑ Starts to experiment with the amount of force needed to pick up different objects

- ❑ Responding to information from muscles and joints to learn about moving in and out of positions; as well as balance and movement in one position such as when rocking back and forth on hands and knees

. . . .

DID YOU KNOW?

Babies as young as 7 months old understand behaviors in the same way adults do and will mirror other's behaviors, so baby is already learning to imitate you.

. . . .

SAFETY "PINS"

▫ Ensure that any sharp edges or corners on nearby furniture are covered.

▫ Baby proof or lock all low cupboards and doors if you haven't already.

▫ The American Academy of Pediatrics recommends **never to use baby walkers.** They are related to many injuries and can eliminate the desire to walk. This led to the development of exersaucers. **Refer to developmental information and recommendations in Month 6 chapter on exersaucers (as well as bouncers and jumpers).**

What can I do to help support my baby's development at this age?

▫ As baby works into sitting more and more, he will split most of his play time between tummy and sitting. Continue to encourage tummy time play, and transitional movements—getting in and out of sit, getting onto hands and knees, and any free movement play on the floor.

▫ Weight bearing on hands will be happening more and more between 7-9 months. Whether pushing up when on tummy, on hands and knees, or supporting himself while moving through positions, this is strengthening his arms but he is also lengthening the muscles and tissues of his palm and fingers, and developing the arches of the hands in preparation for future fine motor skills.

▫ Try putting baby blocks or shapes in a pan of gelatin to dig out for messy sensory play.

- More messy play with purees or with baby safe/edible paint such as yogurt with food coloring. Try with baby in just his diaper and sitting on a large plastic cloth, in the bath tub, or in a baby pool for easier cleanup, and a whole body sensory experience with messy play.

- Water play—in the bath tub or simply place a few inches of water in a pan for baby to reach in to get items

- Sensory bags and bottles as in previous chapters. Use painter's tape to fasten sensory bags to the wall to play and explore the bag in sitting or supported standing as well as on tummy. Baby may also like to bat at water with food coloring in different bags, sealed and taped to the wall, to watch the water splash within the bag and feel how it "squishes".

- Give baby a wet cloth to help wipe his tray or his face.

- Feeling and exploring different textures of clothing during dressing or laundry—talk about colors, texture, and name items

- Toys with buttons baby can push easily to activate for cause and effect

- Stacking/nesting cups and toys, activity cubes, and putting in/taking out of containers

- Babies love to explore household object at this age. She will enjoy being in the kitchen with you—playing with bowls, lids, measuring cups and other safe items. For example, giving her a large bowl helps her figure out how to use both hands together to lift it or turn it over, or to get out other bowls that are stacked within a large bowl.

- Let baby get exposure to some real foods such as holding, feeling, and exploring the shapes of melon, squash, orange, grapefruit or apple for example.

- Bubbles, balls, and blocks! She may not be able to make a big stack of blocks yet but will love to watch you build so she can knock them down.

- Continue to talk, narrate, sing, read and tell stories. Exposing your baby to lots of words is a tool you can use wherever you go!

- Incorporate hand puppets or stuffed animals into your reading, songs, or stories.

- Offer choices, holding up two items at a time—2 books, 2 shirts, or 2 toys for example. Ask "do you want ___ or ___?" and baby may reach for, point, or gaze at his choice, as well as vocalize.

- Look through family pictures with baby, name people and talk about them.

- Mirror play—silly faces, imitate movements, or peek-a-boo moving in/out of mirror image

- Musical instrument toys and sound activated/musical toys (cause and effect)

- Continue to have a variety of teethers and teething items as baby continues to explore with his mouth.

- Movement play—safely holding and gently moving baby through the air—side to side, up and down, upside-down, dancing and turning in a circle. With a beach-ball or similar size, you can support baby on tummy over the ball and move forward and back and side to side. When she places her hands to the floor as the ball is moved forward, she is working on building upper body strength and as well as her core muscles. She will also enjoy bouncing on your lap and bouncing in standing.

- Outside play and exploration—talk about and feel baby safe things you can find outside. Point out items and talk about the sounds (birds, dog barking, car going by, or a lawnmower for example)

- Have baby join you as a part of mealtimes in her high chair. Even if she is not eating at the time she will benefit from being around the sights, sounds, and smells of food, and observe and learn how others eat at mealtime.

- Join your baby in doing "nothing"—remember to pause and see what she initiates. She may want to "talk" back and forth, cuddle with you, or take the lead to get you to do a certain action.

Examples of concerns you may want to talk with your health care provider about,—if your baby:

- Refuses to cuddle or can't be comforted
- Doesn't roll over
- Doesn't bear weight on legs
- Doesn't sit while supported
- Doesn't reach for objects
- Doesn't babble or make a variety of sounds
- Doesn't show response to sounds or has limited response to sounds
- Isn't interested in toys, books, pictures or playful interactions with others
- Doesn't have equal motion with eye movement or eyes aren't equal when focusing on something
- Has difficulty eating or drinking
- Doesn't follow objects with both eyes
- Uses only one side of the body to move
- Is unable to be calmed
- Seems too stiff or too floppy in body or limbs
- Doesn't show affection for parents and caregivers

NOTES

8

MONTHS

. . .

BABY'S SUPERPOWER

—

Enthusiastic Explorer

FINE MOTOR

- ❑ Rakes objects up with thumb side of the hand

- ❑ Grasps small finger food item with thumb against side of curled index finger and may start to grasp a small piece of food with thumb and tip of index or middle finger

- ❑ Uses a complete grasp around a block with thumb and fingers

- ❑ When holding an object in each hand and presented with a 3rd, baby will drop one object to pick up the 3rd

- ❑ Tries to poke with index finger (may have all fingers extended)

GROSS MOTOR

- ❑ Has a strong desire to spend more time upright

- ❑ Sits unsupported and steady for > 5 minutes

- ❑ Can rotate in sitting or lean forward to get a toy and return to sitting up, maintaining balance

- ❑ Extends one or both arms to support self with open hand to the floor, if loosing balance or falling

- ❑ Doesn't want to stay in one position too long

- ❑ Stands when holding to person or furniture, and may be pulling up to stand

- ❑ Gets into a crawling position and creeps on hands and knees, and may sometimes still pull self along the floor with arms (army crawl)

- ❑ Rotates to a sitting position from lying on back and then to quadruped (hands and knees)

SOCIAL-EMOTIONAL

- ❏ May develop stranger anxiety and separation anxiety

- ❏ Plays peek-a-boo back and forth with you—baby may initiate on your request or repeat to try to get a reaction from you

- ❏ Prefers to be with people

- ❏ Laughs and smiles at playful singing and games, such as pat-a-cake or peeking around an object

- ❏ Demands social attention

- ❏ May become attached to a comfort object such as a stuffed animal or a blanket

COMMUNICATION

- ❏ Looks for family members or pets when named

- ❏ Understands "no-no"

- ❏ Produces long chains of repeated consonant/vowel combinations

- ❏ Begins to connect sounds/words to actual ideas and objects that can be universally understood. For example, when baby hears the word "milk," she knows she will get bottle or breast soon.

- ❏ Babbles consonant/vowel combinations perceived as a word by others —"dada" or "mama"

- ❏ Shouts or gets loud for attention

- ❏ Imitates babbling sounds an adult makes

- ❏ Produces sounds without having to move body

- ❏ Babbles multiple syllables using m, n, t, d, b, p, y (6-9 months)

SELF-HELP

- ❏ Begins to eat thicker baby food cereals and thicker purees– Stage 2 type foods (no chunks yet). Thicker foods will help lay the foundation for handling a solid piece of food, as baby will need to use her tongue and mouth muscles more with thicker purees.

- ❏ This may also be a time that parents introduce first finger foods, although many infants are ready closer to 9 months. It is important to start with **MELTABLE solids which are defined as food which will dissolve with saliva only and minimal pressure,** such as baby puffs. These are safe for baby because of the meltable quality, but the initial firmness helps him learn and get experience with beginning chewing and moving a food item around the mouth to prepare for swallowing. The little prongs of the puffs can be broken off as a smaller piece to start with. Items like Cheerios are NOT meltable solids. Try it—compare how long a Cheerio versus a puff melts in your mouth with spit only and minimal pressure of tongue to the roof of your mouth. If baby gets a meltable like a puff in his mouth and doesn't initiate munching or mashing it, it will melt into his saliva so he can swallow it without difficulty. **Also see recommendations of what baby should accomplish before moving to stage 3 foods (the kind with individual chunks or mixed textures) in the next chapter—9 months.** The primary source of nutrition is still breast milk or formula. Purees and meltables are "extras" helping baby learn about food, how to feed himself, and develop oral motor skills needed for successful feeding.

❑ Feeding

- **Breast-fed:** Every 3-4 hours until baby is satisfied.

- **Bottle-fed:** 6-8 ounces, 4-5 times/day

- **Solid food:** 6-8 ounces 3 times/day, and two 2-ounce snacks (thicker baby food cereals and thicker smooth purees—Stage 2 type)

***When introducing a new food, look for signs of a food allergy (rashes, diarrhea, vomiting, irritability, breathing difficulties) while sticking with that food for 3-5 days before introducing a different new food. You may also want to ask your pediatrician for any recommended medications to have on hand in case baby does have an allergic reaction, or other medication needs such as in the case of a fever.

For more information on allergies visit www.foodallergy.org

Gagging from 8-10 months is normal when baby is trying new tastes and textures. When your baby gags, it is best to stay calm and not scare him by panicking. Try to remain neutral in emotion and talk to your baby about what is happening, such as "oh, I see that went too far back—use your tongue like this", then model moving tongue side to side as if you are moving a piece of food or model chewing motions. If you need to assist physically with helping move food in the mouth, do it in a calm and slow manner as we don't want to cause fear in eating and let him know "Mommy/Daddy will help you". Of course infant/child CPR is important to know too!

❑ **See cup and straw drinking information in Month 6 chapter**

❑ Sleeps about 11 hours at night (many straight through) and naps 3-4 hours during the day split between 2 naps.

❑ Enjoys bath time, plays and splashes

COGNITIVE AND PLAY

- ❑ Repeats enjoyable activities

- ❑ Attains a partially hidden object

- ❑ Responds to name being called

- ❑ May start to put items in containers after shown

- ❑ Knows whether an object is near or far

- ❑ Starts to notice the size of objects, reaching for smaller objects with finger and thumb and larger objects with both hands

- ❑ Understands that shapes are different

VISUAL

- ❑ Can see well across a room but still sees things better close up versus further away

- ❑ Further developing depth perception

- ❑ Pats, smiles at, and may try to kiss a mirror

- ❑ Responds to peek-a-boo with enjoyment and repeating

VISUAL-MOTOR

- ❑ Bangs toys and other things together

- ❑ Visually targets, picks up and feeds self finger foods

- ❑ Pokes index finger into holes

- ❑ Eye-hand coordination is further enhanced with crawling on hands and knees

SENSORY

❑ Continues to explore textures and shape of toys and objects

❑ Explores texture, smell, and taste of safe finger foods

❑ Uses sense of smell to help decide whether he/she likes new foods

❑ Develops taste preferences for foods

❑ Able to identify direction of sounds and recognize familiar words

❑ Recognizes familiar textures such as a favorite blanket

❑ Observes environment from a variety of positions— lying on back or tummy, sitting, crawling and standing with assistance, but often prefers being upright

❑ Enjoys a variety of movement in play or when being carried

. . . .

DID YOU KNOW?

It can take 10 or more tries/tastes before
baby decides he likes a new food.

. . . .

- Make sure baby's crib is away from windows. If there are cords on windows—make sure they are removed or tied up high out of baby's reach to prevent strangling.

What can I do at this age to help support my baby's development?

- Make sure to involve baby in mealtimes so she can watch you eat, smell the food and get exposed to what different foods look like. Provide some of her purees on her tray to explore.

- At this stage, your baby thinks making noise is fun! Take turns with silly noises, and copy baby's sounds/noises.

- Toy instruments or household items such as a wooden spoon and plastic bowl to turn into a "drum"—imitate each other

- Sing, dance and clap to the beat with music

- Baby might enjoy rain stick type toys like this found at, https://tinyurl.com/y6ohqel4.

- Help your little one stand during play such as at an activity table, or with a favorite toy on an ottoman, bench or couch—a height where he can easily still play with a toy or look at a book while you help him stand.

- Place favorite items a little out of reach to encourage crawling. As he progresses with this, place pillows and toys for him to maneuver around or over; or a tunnel or large box (opened on both ends) to crawl through. Crawling on grass or other outside surfaces gives a different sensory experience, as does just being outside and exploring!

- You can start teaching your baby simple sign language as early as 8 months, such as signs for "more" or "all done", still saying the word while doing the sign. Baby will first understand the signs and meaning before imitating and using them in later months. Incorporating signs promotes language development, and can reduce frustrations by giving baby an early means of communicating their needs before he or she is able to use words. There are books with baby signs as well as videos and websites such as http://www.babysignlanguage.com and http://www.signingtimes.com.

- Reading, talking, singing, telling stories all continue to be very important to baby's language development. Continuing to talk about what you are doing and what baby is doing is helpful as well as starting to name feelings—"you seem sad", " I know that makes you mad", "you are so happy!" or talking about your feelings—"I am so tired right now".

- Baby will want to look at books on his own too. This is great for early literacy skills and learning fine motor skills to position the book, turn pages, or hold with both hands.

- Have a variety of teethers and teething toys as baby continues to explore with his mouth.

- Bubbles and balls are probably still favorites!

- Water play—inside or out. It can be as simple as a few stacking cups and a container of water. Have a few floating things so that baby learns how to grasp objects that move or as they floats away—she will be using her eyes and hands to work together to get the object.

- Another fun sensory experience is to play with a bowl full of cooked spaghetti. You can also use food coloring and make a variety of colored noodles. There are many recipes online such as this: https://www.messylittlemonster.com/2017/03/how-to-make-rainbow-spaghetti-sensory-play.html. Baby will feel the sticky, squishy texture, watch how the noodles flop around, and will be using lots of hand and finger skills in manipulating the spaghetti. Try with baby just in his diaper. Place a noodle on his shoulder and say "uh oh there's a noodle on your shoulder". See if he can figure out how to get it off. Then you can move to naming other body parts—"now it's on your tummy" (your arm, your leg, etc.) He may enjoy this over the next months too!

- Place familiar objects in front of baby and ask "Where's the book?"... your puppy?, the ball?, the spoon?, etc. Get excited when she picks the right one!

- Baby is really exploring items with her hands now. She will like things she can bang, drop, or throw, or get out of containers. Provide a variety of shapes, sizes and textures through her toys (blocks, rings on stacking pole, nesting toys, activity cubes, cause and effect toys)but she will also still enjoy exploring safe items in the kitchen (bowls, lids, cups, whisk, wooden or silicone spatulas, strainers).

- Place ribbons through holes punched into a flexible plastic container lid with knots on each end of the ribbon so they can't be pulled through the holes. Your little one can then pull on the ribbons from either side, and will be really working her hand and finger skills. You can also try this using the holes of a colander.

- "Sticky wall fun": Use painter's tape to tape contact paper to a wall with the sticky side out, at level for baby in sitting. Stick some chunky puzzle pieces or other blocks and shapes to it for baby to work her fine motor skills to pull them off.

Examples of concerns you may want to talk with your health care provider about,—if your baby:

- Has difficulty eating or drinking

- Doesn't babble or make a variety of sounds

- Doesn't maintain eye contact during playful interaction

- Is not interested in interacting with others

- Doesn't try to move to get toys

- Does not enjoy different types of movement

- Doesn't have equal motion with eye movement or eyes aren't equal when focusing on something
- Doesn't transfer toys from one hand to the other
- Doesn't bear full weight on legs
- Doesn't show response to sounds or has limited response to sounds
- Isn't interested in toys, books, or pictures
- Uses one side of the body significantly more than the other
- Is unable to calm or be comforted

NOTES

9

MONTHS

• • •

BABY'S SUPERPOWER

———

Master of Jabber

FINE MOTOR

- ❑ Picks up small objects with fingertip of index finger and thumb (pincer grasp)
- ❑ Releases objects intentionally—may drop or throw
- ❑ Puts objects into container
- ❑ Waves "bye-bye"
- ❑ Can hold one item in each hand at the same time
- ❑ Bangs 2 objects together
- ❑ Reaches overhead in sitting
- ❑ Pokes index finger into hole (such as hole in pegboard)
- ❑ Turns several pages of a board book at once

GROSS MOTOR

- ❑ Can sit for 10 minutes or more independently
- ❑ Can lean forward or to the sides in sitting and return to sitting upright
- ❑ May try to scoot on her bottom
- ❑ Gets into hands and knees position and crawls forward on hands and knees
- ❑ Changes from a crawling position back into a sitting position
- ❑ Pulls to standing at furniture
- ❑ Starting to cruise along furniture (side-stepping while holding to furniture)

❑ Plays some in kneeling and ½ kneeling

❑ Climbs some stairs but cannot back down

SOCIAL-EMOTIONAL

❑ Responds playfully in front of a mirror

❑ Smiles at own mirror image

❑ Shows anxiety over separation from mother

❑ Often can clap hands together

❑ Enjoys interactive games such as "so big" (baby imitates or puts arms up when you say "so big")

❑ Seeks reassurance from caregivers

❑ May attach to a favorite blanket or stuffed animal, using as a "transitional object" for security

❑ Responds to expressions of emotion from other people

❑ Reaches to be picked up and held

COMMUNICATION

❑ Responds to simple requests when combined with gestures

❑ Begins to use hand movements or gestures to communicate wants and needs—pointing or reaching toward

❑ Looks at familiar objects and people when named

❑ Responds to own name

- ❑ Temporarily responds to "no-no" by stopping the action

- ❑ Shows recognition of commonly used words, and the meaning of some facial expressions and tone of voice

- ❑ Waves "bye-bye"

- ❑ Babbles using several consonants

- ❑ Imitates sounds

- ❑ Says "mama" and dada" (but may say to others, not just parents)

SELF-HELP

- ❑ Holds bottle independently if bottle fed

- ❑ Sits upright independently in high chair

- ❑ Moves trunk forward to bring mouth to the spoon, and uses lips to remove food from spoon when interested in the food

- ❑ Sleeps about 11 hours at night (many straight through) and naps about 3 hours during the day split between 2 naps.

- ❑ If disinterested in food, will keep mouth closed, and lean or turn away

- ❑ Finger feeds self

- ❑ Feeding

    - **Breast-fed:** On demand or every 3-4 hours until baby is content or satisfied.

    - **Bottle-fed:** 6-8 ounces, 4-5 times/day

    - **Solid food 6-8 ounces 3 times/day, and two 2-ounce snacks**

***When introducing a new food, look for signs of a food allergy (rashes, diarrhea, vomiting, irritability, breathing difficulties) while sticking with that food for 3-5 days before introducing a different new food. You may also want to ask your pediatrician for any recommended medications to have on hand in case baby does have an allergic reaction, or other medication needs such as in the case of a fever.*

For more information on allergies visit www.foodallergy.org

If baby has managed thicker baby food purees (like Stage 2's), then it is time to try some soft mashed table foods or pureed table foods. Per my training in sensory processing, oral motor skills and the SOS (sequential oral sensory) Approach to Feeding, I follow the recommendations NOT to move to a Stage 3 food that has mixed textures, until baby is able to successfully chew and swallow a single texture. For more information, visit sosapproachtofeeding.com.

Some Stage 3 foods are purees with chunks in them. When baby takes a spoonful of a mixed texture, she may perceive the puree as something she only needs to suck off the spoon and doesn't need to chew, and will then move the food back for a swallow only to be startled by a chunk food that may cause gagging and a negative response to further trying foods. Therefore once she accomplishes moving a variety of single textures (1 piece at a time) around her mouth to successfully chew and swallow, she then will be ready to detect chunks in mixed textures and be able to move them to her teeth to chew, even though some of the pureed part may be swallowed first.

Your baby may have already tried meltable solids such as the baby puffs. These are the starting point for feeling food that is initially hard in the mouth to trigger chewing and tongue movement to move the food around the mouth and prepare for a swallow. The meltable solids are a safe starting point, because they dissolve with spit only and very minimal pressure. Even before starting a meltable solid, baby can benefit from supervised exploration with *safe, longer, harder food items that baby **cannot** break or bite off,* such as a full size thick carrot, or celery stalk, and the item should be long enough so that it cannot fit all the way into baby's mouth. She needs to be able to have a good amount of the item to grasp and hold outside of her mouth while moving the other end all around her mouth. This may seem counter-intuitive, but the goal is exploration ONLY, and doing so with real food. It helps baby experiment with gumming on the sides of her mouth but also working on tongue movement following the food around her mouth, which is needed to move food in your mouth side to side and onto the teeth, to complete chewing. Baby should **ALWAYS BE SUPERVISED** when trying this exploration and with any new foods. She is also learning how to control her hand movements to coordinate with moving food in, out and around her mouth.

After successfully managing meltables (9—10 months) baby would then next move to trying single pieces of soft cubes (about the size of ½ your pinky nail), such as avocado, Gerber Graduate fruits, overcooked squash pieces, kiwi, bananas, or the single vegetable pieces out of soup (removed from the broth), soft sweet potato or regular potato cubes. They should soften even more as you heat them up, but do test the pieces to make sure they are very soft as this may vary from brand to brand. As baby allows, you can place a single piece to the molar area to cue her to initiate chewing.

Your little one may want to take food out of her mouth to inspect or put back in. Or maybe she didn't like it and she is just trying to get the food out of her mouth. Letting her remove food or spit food out is an important part of letting her feel safe! Imagine biting into a piece of food and you discovered something unpleasant or unsafe about it, yet you were not unable to spit it out.

Baby may have been practicing open cup and straw drinking for a while now and has possibly mastered it! If not, **refer to Month 6 chapter on introducing cup and straw drinking under Self Help Skills. 9 months is a good time to introduce the straw if baby wasn't previously ready.** Always make sure baby is sitting upright well in her chair when attempting to drink. It is best to start with a think puree then move to sips of breast milk or formula, and water when your pediatrician says it's ok to give sips of water. At 9 months baby may be holding the cup by herself or with assistance. Cups with handles are sometimes easier to start with than ones without handles. It is good to continue to have baby take sips from an open cup as well. Doing both straw cup and open cup will help her develop the oral motor skills she needs to drink from a variety of containers. As mentioned previously, babies often drink from a straw by 9 months, and some as early as 6-8months. Little ones typically master independent open cup drinking by 18 months, being able to grade the tipping of the cup to control the flow, take in appropriate amount of liquid for swallowing and have rare spilling.

COGNITIVE AND PLAY

❑ Works for and problem solves how to get desired objects that are out of reach

❑ Touches toy or adult's hand to restart an activity

❑ Searches briefly for an object when it's taken away

❑ Understands how objects can be used—bang blocks to make noise, shake a rattle, or push buttons on a toy

❑ May look for a remembered toy in remembered location or look for a person hidden behind something

❑ Notices the size of objects, reaching for larger objects with both hands and smaller ones with thumb and fingers

❑ Takes items in/out of containers

❑ Looks at familiar objects and people when named

❑ Follows some routine verbal requests when paired with gestures

VISUAL

❑ After seeing an object covered by a cloth, picks up the cloth

❑ Looks at simple pictures when they are named

❑ Depth perception has continued to improve and baby can generally judge distance pretty well

❑ Looks at pages of a book while you read

❑ Shows interest in pictures

VISUAL-MOTOR

❑ Imitates simple actions such as banging an object on table

❑ Looks at and feels what is in a container

❑ Pulls on a string to get a toy

❑ Picks up, pushes, or shoves fairly large objects

❑ Crawling is helping hand-eye coordination develop

SENSORY

❑ Increase in smell preference and reaction

❑ Enjoys a greater variety of tastes

❑ Recognizes and reacts to certain songs and sounds—loves familiar voices

❑ Gets increased touch and pressure input to palms with creeping on hands and knees and grasping many objects

❑ Investigates shapes, sizes and textures with hands and explores with mouth

❑ Observes environment from a variety of positions, but prefers to be upright

❑ Experiments with the amount of force needed to pick up different objects, such as recognizing need for a stronger grasp for heavier objects

❑ Can self calm when riding in car if not tired or hungry

. . . .

DID YOU KNOW?

Baby's eyes are typically their final color at this time.

. . . .

□ Never leave baby unsupervised when playing with things she may put in her mouth. Don't give baby any hard pieces of food or pieces of a size that could block her airway. It is a good idea to learn infant/child CPR so you will know what to do if baby is ever choking.

What can I do at this age to help support my baby's development?

□ As baby is crawling more, have her try crawling on different textured surfaces, through tunnels, or over pillows or cushions. There are many developmental benefits to crawling—developing bilateral coordination, weight bearing on hands lengthening hand/finger muscles, helping arches of the hands develop; integrating reflexes, developing postural control and motor planning skills, and much more. *Even after toddlers are walking, they can benefit from continued play on hands and knees.*

□ Boxes opened on both ends and taped together with "windows" cut out make fun tunnels and you can play a little peek-a-boo along the way. You can hang silky ribbons or socks for example from the box tops to create sensory exploration or serve as items for her to reach for and pull through the holes.

□ Drop blocks or other items into metal bowl or pan to experiment with different objects making different sounds.

□ Place items all around baby in sitting to encourage reaching across her body to reach for an object to place in a container in front of her, OR when she picks up the objects, move the container around in different positions for her to reach and drop the item in.

- Roll a ball to your baby and see if she stops it or tries to push it back toward you. You can say things like "ready, set, go!" when you roll the ball and soon baby will anticipate the ball coming toward her when she hears this.

- Music and clapping, nursery rhymes and singing; and singing songs, with actions such as "Itsy bitsy spider", or incorporate pictures or puppets along with your songs

- Continue to read daily to your baby—name pictures and talk about them. Feel textures of items and in books, naming the textures—soft, bumpy, rough.

- Continue to talk to baby about what you are doing, what baby is exploring, and label emotions as they arise. Remember to create those pauses for baby to respond or initiate communication and back-and-forth exchanges with you.

- Offer choices during daily activities such as holding up 2 choices of food and asking baby which one he wants; or 2 shirts during dressing, and asking baby "do you want to wear green or blue?" for example. Baby may point or reach for her preference, or try to vocalize her choice.

- When baby starts to pull to stand: Stand up at an activity table or stand up to play with favorite toys or books on the couch, ottoman, or coffee table. Leave room for baby to try to begin cruising along furniture and space out motivating toys/items to each side of him to encourage cruising toward a toy out of reach. Cruising is just taking those first side-to-side steps while holding to something for support. This typically happens after baby has achieved pulling himself up to stand. It is a step in gaining the strength and skills in standing that baby needs to eventually let go of that support.

- Demonstrate how buttons or knobs work on toys and see if baby imitates you.

- Water play and messy play—in the bath tub, on a tray in the kitchen or take it outside. Baby will like toys, cups and things he can play with in the water. Splash, scoop up and dump water out of cups; or try to squeeze water out of sponges.

▫ More messy sensory play with pudding painting, or painting in the bathtub with edible paints (yogurt with natural food coloring for example), or find items hidden in flour or oatmeal in a pan or tray.

▫ Use a food processor to make finely ground up "sand" out of taste safe items such as graham crackers. Place some cups or other items in the "sand" for baby to explore.

▫ Try a "Jell-O dig"—letting a few cookie cutters or toys set up in a pan of gelatin and baby has to dig to get them out.

▫ pipSquigz (https://tinyurl.com/yxp82yrh) and pipSquigz Ringlets (https://tinyurl.com/y495vxal) to work on grasping and pulling, giving baby an opportunity to strengthen his hands and grade the amount of force needed to remove the pipSquigz which can be suctioned together or to different surfaces—high chair tray when sitting, or window/glass door in sitting or standing. When doing it in standing he will be strengthening and using his arms differently, as well as being challenged with his balance. If not standing well yet, try it next month!

▫ Outdoors: so much sensory input and so much to explore—different every season! Have baby feel nature items as you name them, talk about how they feel, how they smell, what color they are, or what something sounds like. Point out and name many things as you go on a walk. Baby may also point at things that grasp her attention. Talk about things related to the weather—hot, cold, wet, sunny, or rainy.

▫ Various stacking items such as cups and stacking rings on a pole

▫ Different sizes and shapes of blocks to stack or put in/out of containers

▫ Empty wipe containers or empty tissue boxes to pull silky scarfs up through the opening

▫ Ball drop toys, such as those with holes and ramps. You can also talk about the colors of the balls and make noises such as "zoooom!" as the balls go down the ramp.

▫ Toys with buttons and knobs, such as on activity tables or cubes

▫ Stuff pompoms in a whisk and let baby use his pincer grasp (thumb and pointer finger together) and problem solve to get them out. This is also great for coordinating the use of both hands together, using one to stabilize the whisk and the other to get out the pompoms.

- Kitchen: Baby will still like to explore cupboards, opening and closing doors. Keep unsafe items out of reach and child proof locks on cupboards as needed, but you may choose to leave one cupboard or drawer unlocked with safe items such as plastic containers, measuring cups, and wooden spoons or bowls available for baby to access and play with while joining you in the kitchen.

- During Dressing: Talk or sing about body parts and clothing—"let's put your arm in the shirt", "the shirt goes over your head", "socks go over your toes to keep your foot warm".

- When folding laundry, hide under a towel or sheet and see if baby pulls it off to "find" you. Let baby feel different textures of clothing, pull clothing items out of a basket (sitting or standing at the basket), or toss in the basket. Later on when able, baby can work on squatting to pick something up, then return to stand to drop in the basket.

- When at the grocery store, hold up and name food items you are getting and let baby feel some of the items. You can name foods and talk about the colors, or if an item is cold or wet such as some produce. Baby will also be exposed to the different smells such as in the bakery or items near the deli.

- You may choose to use baby sign language as mentioned in Month 8 to encourage communication.

- Place meltables like puffs in an egg carton or ice cube tray compartments for an added challenge to fine motor skills

- Place colorful washi tape or painters tape on baby's tray, a pan, or on the floor encourage fine motor skills and using thumb and index finger together for a pincher grasp. You can keep one end folded over as a starting spot for baby to pull easier. Of course always watch what baby puts in his mouth!

Examples of concerns you may want to talk with your health care provider about,—if your baby:

- Seems unusually quiet or does not vocalize

- Doesn't babble sounds like "mama", "baba" and "dada"

- Has difficulties with feedings, and transition to purees

- Does not look toward sounds or respond to his/her name

- Avoids eye contact

- Is persistently unable to calm

- Seems unusually stiff or floppy in body or extremities

- Cannot take weight on legs

- Doesn't transfer toys from one hand to the other

- Doesn't sit with propping or holding

- Doesn't look where you point

- Isn't interested in toys, books, or pictures

- Uses one side of the body significantly more than the other

- Does not enjoy different types of movement such as being swung or lifted into the air, or gets upset in certain positions such as lying back for diaper changes

- Has difficulty with eating or drinking

NOTES

10

MONTHS

• • •

BABY'S SUPERPOWER

—

Curious Copycat

FINE MOTOR

- ❑ Grasps small objects easily using thumb to index finger tip (pincer grasp)

- ❑ Able to isolate index finger to point (with other fingers flexed)

- ❑ Squeezes a squeaking toy with either hand

- ❑ Purposefully pulls a string attached to an object to move it closer

- ❑ Places an object on a flat surface with voluntary release

- ❑ Can hold a small object in 1 hand while crawling

- ❑ Uses both hands equally to play and explore toys

GROSS MOTOR

- ❑ Sits for long periods

- ❑ Moves in and out of sitting easily

- ❑ Crawls on hands and knees independently

- ❑ Pulls self to stand and cruises along furniture

- ❑ Reaches for an object in front or to either side with one hand while supporting weight on other hand/arm

- ❑ May stand unsupported for 5 seconds

- ❑ Makes stepping movements with hands held (and sometimes only one hand held)

- ❑ Able to lower into sitting from standing at furniture

❑ Demonstrates good balance reactions in sitting and starts to catch self with arms/hands if losing balance backward in sitting

❑ Kneels without support

❑ Climbs up some stairs,—may look behind and lower to sit on hip on stair but still needs assistance to back down

SOCIAL-EMOTIONAL

❑ Waves "bye-bye" or may blow kisses

❑ Plays pat-a-cake

❑ Gives affection

❑ May continue with signs of separation anxiety

❑ Generally happy when not hungry or tired

❑ Reaches arms to be picked up

❑ Imitates other children and mimics simple actions

❑ Develops confidence that he can finger feed himself

COMMUNICATION

❑ Can understand and follow simple requests such as "wave bye-bye", "clap hands", or "give me the toy"

❑ Baby may point to or reach toward an object that you name

❑ Produces longer strings of jargon in social communication with more intonation

❑ Explores different sounds that he/she can make and imitates sounds

❑ May correctly refer to each parent as "mama or "dada"

SELF-HELP SKILLS

❑ Typically enjoys bath time and playing in the water

❑ Usually tolerates diaper changes without crying

❑ Often can calm self to fall asleep

❑ Able to finger feed more successfully

❑ Able to bite and chew soft food pieces and meltable solids

❑ May want to play with spoon at mealtimes and bring to mouth

❑ Holds bottle independently and tips up independently

❑ Assists with cup drinking and spoon feeding

  ▫ Baby may be using a straw cup or 360 drinking cup well now

  ▫ **See cup and straw drinking information in Month 6 chapter**

❑ Feeding

- **Breast-fed:** On demand or every 3-4 hours until baby is content or satisfied.

- **Bottle-fed:** 6-8 ounces, 3-5 times/day

- **Solid food:** 3 meals and two 2-ounce snacks per day

***When introducing a new food, look for signs of a food allergy (rashes, diarrhea, vomiting, irritability, breathing difficulties) while sticking with that food for 3-5 days before introducing a different new food. You may also want to ask your pediatrician for any recommended medications to have on hand in case baby does have an allergic reaction, or other medication needs such as in the case of a fever.*

For more information on allergies visit www.foodallergy.org

❑ Baby typically is trying different *soft cube foods* as talked about in Month 9 chapter, and may do so throughout month 10. Next up as he approaches 11 months, he will move to what we call *soft mechanical SINGLE textures*—so just one more texture type to master before doing those mixed textures such as a Stage 3 type food with chunks! Soft mechanical single textures are foods that are still soft and break up easily, but require a bit more chewing such as baby bite size pieces of muffin, very soft pasta, lunch meat in cubes, thin deli meat cut into small rectangle, scrambled eggs, or soft sweet potato cubes.

❑ Sleeps 10-12 hours at night and naps about 3 hours during the day split between 2 naps. Morning naps may taper off.

COGNITIVE AND PLAY

❑ Puts objects in and out of containers

❑ Explores objects in many different ways (shaking, banging, turning, throwing, dropping)

❑ Begins to use familiar objects in the correct function (spoon to mouth, comb to hair)—imitates you using common, frequently used objects (toy phone to ear)

❑ Retains 2 objects in hand and reaches for a 3rd

❑ Starting to understand and learn spatial relationships, especially if talked about in play—on/off, up/down, under/over

❑ Turns pages in a book

VISUAL

❑ Looks closely at tiny objects

❑ Gazes at or in the direction of a named object

❑ Able to better focus on quickly moving objects

❑ Looks at and scans pages of book as you read

VISUAL-MOTOR

❑ Removes items from containers, picking
things out or dumping them out

❑ Imitates using 2 different objects, such as hitting a cup with a spoon

❑ Slides an object, (like a car) on a surface

❑ Claps hands several times

❑ Pulls on a string to get the attached toy

❑ Releases a block into an adult's held out palm

SENSORY

❑ Enjoys a greater variety of tastes

❑ Developing food preferences—may take 10 tries
before baby learns to like a new food

❑ Baby is getting around more, and therefore exploring
textures through touching a variety of objects and surfaces

❑ Enjoys and explores a wide variety of touch, noises and smells

❑ Usually does not startle to everyday sounds

❑ Able to calm with rocking, holding, and to your voice or singing

❑ Increase in smell and taste preference, and intensity of reaction

❑ Continues to investigates shapes, sizes and textures
with hands and explores with mouth

❑ Observes environment from a variety of positions and enjoys
playful movement in different directions and positions

DID YOU KNOW?

Newborns don't have knee caps. Well sort of.....The knee cap, also known as the patella, is soft cartilage at birth and doesn't develop into hard bone until 3-5 years of age.

- ☐ Make sure any furniture baby can pull up on is secure to where the furniture or items cannot be pulled off or fall on top of baby.

What can I do at this age to help support my baby's development?

- ☐ Help put words to baby's actions: "(Baby's name) is all done eating"—when refusing or pushing away food. "I see you are tired"—when sleepy and reaching for blanket. "That's your favorite toy. Let's play!"—when reaching for or playing with favorite toy.

- ☐ Sensory play—continued water play, messy play and exploring textures and items outdoors as well—sand, dirt, grass. Baby may continue to enjoy different sensory bags mentioned previously. Doing messy play in the bath tub, a baby pool, or on a plastic cloth can all help with clean up.

- ☐ Wallet or purse play—babies love to pull things out of a purse or wallet, feel zippers and snaps, and explore pockets. Use an old one, and place a few of baby's items inside to explore (make sure any coins or other unsafe items have been removed). One option is to place playing cards or cut cardstock to fit in the credit card slots. This would allow baby to work on using his fingertips to get them out, further developing fine motor skills.

- ☐ Request baby to do familiar actions—"let's dance", "wave bye bye", "show me So Big!", and model as needed.

▫ Music, dancing, clapping, singing, and songs with actions

▫ Encourage your little one to imitate you playing or doing actions, and imitate her in return. Try it in front of a mirror!

▫ Mealtimes: Let baby be a part of your mealtimes or watch meal prep whenever possible. It allows him to be around the smells, sights and sounds and you can let him feel and explore foods. Example—let him see and touch an un-husked corn cob, watch you husk it and then feel the corn once husked.

▫ As mentioned in month 8 chapter, you may incorporate baby signing for words such as "more", "please", or "eat", when you also say the word. He may not be able to do the sign perfectly but go with his approximation if it is consistent, and continue to model it. He will understand the word and sign before actually being able to do the sign.

▫ Errands and car rides: Talk about and point out all the new things your little one is seeing. Touch, explore, and name items as appropriate during shopping or errands.

▫ Opportunities to play in standing and pull up to standing: place favorite toys on a couch, ottoman, chair, or end table to encourage play in standing. You may spread them out to encourage cruising along the furniture to get to another toy.

▫ Place a bucket or toy (such as a barn for example), on furniture as above, and have items (such as the animals) for baby to squat to floor to reach and then move back up to standing to put the items in the bucket (or barn). This is good to incorporate during toy clean up!

▫ Stick to bare feet at home until baby is actually walking. This helps develop muscles and ligaments in the foot and strengthen the foot's arch. It also helps improve sensory awareness of their position in space, by being able to get necessary sensory input to their feet—not only feeling the surface they are stepping on, but getting input from the muscles and joints in how to respond for balance and weight shift.

▫ Continued opportunities to crawl—try hide and seek! Let baby watch you hide behind the couch for example and then crawl over to find you.

- Shape sorters, stacking items, activity tables, Squigz, toy phone, playing with kitchen items, chunky vehicles baby can push, chunky single piece puzzles, puzzles with knobs to pick up with fingers

- "Sticky wall fun": Place items for baby to pick off. Try pompoms or strings of yarn on the sticky wall—things that will challenge her fingers (fine motor skills). Baby may want to do this in standing but can still do it in sitting too.

- Balls, bubbles, and inflated balloon play (supervised)! *Never let baby play with un-inflated balloons and always be aware if baby is around any balloons that have popped, to carefully look for and pick up any of the balloon pieces to avoid choking.*

- Use painters tape to tape a paper towel core vertically to the wall and show baby how to drop pompom balls of different sizes down the tube onto the floor or maybe into a basket below. You can vary the height to be done in sitting or standing, and later baby can work on squatting to pick up pompom, and returning to stand to drop it in the hole.

- Use painter's tape to tape small farm animals to a wall or tray and have baby peel the tape working on fine motor skills to "rescue" the animals! Doing it on the wall can encourage standing. Tape the animals or other objects to a coffee table and have a basket or the "barn" on the floor for baby to squat and put the animals into. This will encourage a lot of squat to stand movement.

- Loosely weave ribbons through a kitchen whisk for baby to pull out, encouraging problem solving, fine motor skills and bilateral (2-handed) skills.

- Demonstrate simple pretend play and see if baby imitates you such as hugging a baby doll, putting a blanket on doll or stuffed animal, bring a spoon to doll's mouth, or phone up to your ear.

- Baby Wipe Sensory or Picture Boards: There are a lot of options for these! Remove the baby wipe lids from several containers and cut out the inner part, leaving the lid and frame so that the lid can still close. Use a glue gun to secure the lids onto a large piece of cardboard. You can then glue sensory items (pompoms, sand paper, various cloth materials, ribbons, yarn); pictures of familiar objects, or pictures of family members on the cardboard in each frame. Check each item to make sure they are securely attached. Baby can work on opening the lids to find the items. Name the items or people in pictures, and talk about them. You can also write the name of the person or item on the top of the lid.

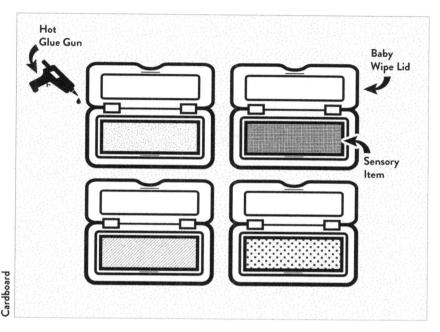

Examples of concerns you may want to talk with your health care provider about,—if your baby:

- Does not seem to use both eyes together well or one eye drifts in or out

- Doesn't babble or imitate sounds

- Does not look toward sounds or respond to his/her name

- Doesn't engage in joyful smiles and back-and-forth interactions with parents/caregivers

- Isn't interested in toys/play and exploring environment

- Has any difficulties with feeding, such as coughing or choking during feeding, or having difficulty transitioning to solids

- Has difficulty sitting for long periods

- Has difficulty crawling

- Seems weaker on one side of body

- Doesn't look where you point

- Is persistently unable to calm

- Doesn't like being moved through the air playfully

- Avoids touching anything messy with his/her hands

NOTES

11

MONTHS

• • •

BABY'S SUPERPOWER

———

Eager Engineer—Interested in How Things Work

FINE MOTOR

❑ Uses a neat pincer grasp (thumb and first finger pads) to pick up small food items, with wrist and arm off of surface or table

❑ Takes objects out of a container and releases object voluntarily

❑ Holds a crayon to paper (typically with whole hand grasp around crayon)

❑ Pokes into holes with an isolated index finger (other fingers tucked out of the way)

❑ Grasps and pulls strongly with one or both hands

❑ Able to tear paper

❑ Manipulates simple toy musical instruments, such banging on drum, using mallet on xylophone or shaking a tambourine

GROSS MOTOR

❑ Cruises well along furniture

❑ With hands held or supported at trunk, takes a few alternating steps forward or in place

❑ Able to hold head upright while crawling

❑ Pivots around in a circle in sitting

❑ Crawls completely over an adults legs

❑ Can stand independently for at least 5 seconds

❑ Lowers self from standing to sitting in a controlled manner

❑ Able to stop a fall or loss of balance in sitting, extending arms backward to support self with open palms

SOCIAL-EMOTIONAL

❑ Extends toy to a person but may not release

❑ Leaves physical contact with a person momentarily

❑ Enjoys interacting with familiar people in play

❑ Performs for social attention—repeats action/ activity that gets a response from others

❑ Imitates facial expressions

❑ May strongly express likes and dislikes, learning to use their emotions to get what they want

❑ May show fear with new situations

COMMUNICATION

❑ Imitates sounds of words

❑ Imitates consonant-vowel combinations

❑ Performs on verbal cue alone (without gesture or modeling)

❑ Imitates non-speech sounds (click, cough)

❑ Baby is learning that words represent a thing, person or action—looks at familiar objects or persons when named

❑ Stops or pauses activity in response to "no"

❑ Engages in back and forth exchanges

❑ Babbling has sounds and rhythms of speech

❑ Refers to "mama" and "dada" correctly

SELF-HELP

- ☐ Removes both socks

- ☐ Helps pull pants down

- ☐ Pushes arms/legs in and out of clothing during dressing

- ☐ Participates in dressing without crying

- ☐ Opens mouth for tooth brushing

- ☐ Feeds self all finger foods, bites and chews

- ☐ Swallows with closed mouth

- ☐ Licks food off of spoon

- ☐ Wants to grasp spoon and will bring to mouth, although may turn upside down

- ☐ Does well during car rides when not tired or hungry

- ☐ Enjoys bath time and plays in bath

- ☐ Enjoys a greater variety of tastes, and lets you know dislikes

- ☐ Holds a cup with both hands to drink with assistance

- ☐ Feeding
  - **Breast-fed:** 3-5 times/day, until baby's content
  - **Bottle-fed:** 6-8 ounces, 2-4 times/day
  - **Solid food:** 3 meals, 2 snacks

- ☐ Sleeps 10-12 hours at night and naps about 2-3 hours during the day split between 2 naps, or may do one longer nap

***When introducing a new food, look for signs of a food allergy (rashes, diarrhea, vomiting, irritability, breathing difficulties) while sticking with that food for 3-5 days before introducing a different new food. You may also want to ask your pediatrician for any recommended medications to have on hand in case baby does have an allergic reaction, or other medication needs such as in the case of a fever.

For more information on allergies visit www.foodallergy.org

❑ Your little one is probably now eating those soft mechanical SINGLE texture foods we talked about last month—foods that are still soft and break up easily, but require a bit more chewing such as baby bite size pieces of muffin, very soft pasta, lunch meat in small cubes, thin deli meat cut into small rectangles, or scrambled eggs. If your little one is handling these well, he will typically continue with these soft mechanical single textures in month 11, and can continue with any soft cubes he likes. Moving into month 12, and if he has been able to successfully manage all previous single textures, he can now move into the soft mechanical textures that are MIXED textures. Because he has mastered the oral motor skills of handling those previous single textures, he should now be able to detect and manage chunks of food within purees or sauces. Besides Stage 3 baby foods with chunks, examples of mixed textures are macaroni and cheese, children's microwaveable meals with food chunks in sauces, spaghetti, lasagna, other casseroles, or a cut up pot pie.

COGNITIVE AND PLAY

- ❑ Imperfectly imitates new movement never performed before

- ❑ Finds and obtains a completely hidden object,
  even if he didn't see you hide the object

- ❑ Takes ring stacks off of a pole

- ❑ Searches for objects inside of a container

- ❑ Learns to make predictions about what is likely to happen based
  on what she's seen and experienced—such as if she sees her diaper
  picked up, she may point to the door thinking it means she is leaving

- ❑ Overcomes obstacles to obtain an object

- ❑ Follows simple requests such as to wave "bye-bye" or reach for a toy

- ❑ Uses familiar objects in the correct function (spoon
  or cup to mouth, comb to hair)—imitates you using
  common, frequently used objects (toy phone to ear)

- ❑ Has longer attention span to focus on play for
  more than a few seconds at a time

VISUAL

- ❑ Finds a small toy after watching you hide it entirely under a cloth

- ❑ Visually tracks a ball rolling down an incline

- ❑ Sees well near and far and can focus on objects moving quickly

- ❑ Can recognize familiar people when looking through a window

- ❑ Recognizes pictures

VISUAL-MOTOR

- ❑ Tries to turn cranks on toys

- ❑ Tries to push or roll a ball away from self

- ❑ Drops small things (raisin sized), into a relatively small opening, such as a cup.

- ❑ Throws things just to see what happens

- ❑ Removes both socks

SENSORY

- ❑ Continues to develop food preferences—may take 10 tries before baby learns to like a new food

- ❑ Enjoys touch of favorite blanket, stuffed animal or toy

- ❑ Starts to investigate objects more through touch than through the mouth

- ❑ Baby's vestibular system (located in the inner ear), vision, and the ability to process information about body position through muscles and joints, and sense of touch are all coordinating together to help him orient in space, balance, and move efficiently to perform a task at hand.

- ❑ Enjoys a wide variety of music/sounds, touch and movement play

- ❑ May turn head away from strong smells

- ❑ Enjoys exploring messy play especially with food

. . . .

DID YOU KNOW?

Babies are born with around 300 bones, 94 more than adults. Some of the bones fuse together as they grow, for a total of 206 as an adult.

SAFETY "PINS"

▫ To reduce accidental drowning, never leave water in the bathtub, or water in large containers or tubs that baby can get into unsupervised. Never leave baby unsupervised in the bath tub or where he can access a swimming pool or body of water. *Drowning is the #1 cause of death in children age 1-4.*

▫ As mentioned before, never let baby play with un-inflated balloons and always be aware if baby is around any balloons that have popped, to carefully look for and pick up any of the balloon pieces to avoid choking.

What can I do at this age to help support my baby's development?

▫ Give baby her own spoon to practice with during mealtimes or if she wants to grab yours help guide her to successfully bring to her mouth. Let her be a part of mealtimes, watching prep while exploring some food on her tray, eating when family eats as much as possible, and observing cleanup. She may enjoy using a wet cloth to help wipe her tray, hands, or face.

▫ Have spoons and cups available in play as well—pretend to stir, feed yourself, feed a doll, or scoop something up, and see if baby imitates

▫ Make time to play with food! This is wonderful exposure without a "requirement" to eat anything. Never force baby to taste or eat anything. When getting items ready for a meal (or after a meal, or really at any time in the kitchen) you can place some items on her tray and be there to supervise and demonstrate. Make a triangle or square with carrot or celery sticks. Stack items. Make a face out of food items with spaghetti or broccoli for hair. There are so many possibilities for baby to have fun while exploring food! Exposure can play a big part in reducing later picky eating. Let him choose if he wants to smell or lick any of the items, as you demonstrate—talk about the feel, the temperature, the colors, the shapes, and the tastes of foods.

□ Baby is understanding "no" so don't be afraid to correct inappropriate or unsafe behaviors but also remember to praise and reinforce any positive behaviors, and catch them doing "good".

□ Let your little one help as much as possible with dressing. Pay attention to what he is initiating and can do—take off socks, pull down shirt, push arms/legs in and out of clothing

□ Also during dressing, name clothing items, colors, and give choices such as "Do you want to wear the green shirt (hold up or point to) or the blue shirt (hold up or point to)".

□ Lay out clothing and say "Let's put on your shirt" or "Give me your pants" to work on following simple requests, and see if he understands and hands you the requested item.

□ You can offer choices in so many situations—at the grocery store, at meal times, choosing a book at bedtime, or choosing a toy at play time.

□ Gather a bunch of hats and take turns putting them on and looking in a mirror.

□ Movement play: Bounce and dance in standing, holding baby's hands as needed. Swinging in safe baby swings, spinning around while you are holding baby, helping baby fly like an airplane. Go for blanket rides!— have baby sit on the blanket and pull him around. Go as slow as you need to so baby can still stay sitting, but this will be working on his balance reactions and stability while responding to changes in speed and changing direction.

□ Encourage standing and squatting activities as mentioned in previous chapters, and if baby is wanting to take steps, she may enjoy learning how she can kick a ball as she walks forward into it, hands held as needed.

▫ Continue to expose baby to a lot of language! Reading, talking, stories, singing, and being silly. Baby may really like the songs with actions! Try pausing in a certain part of the song and see how baby responds. Does he signal to you that he wants you to continue? Tries to fill in song with any sounds or babble, or actions?

▫ When out and about, name colors of things: "The grass is green", "The car is blue", "The ball is red", etc.

▫ Touch and feel board books and books with flaps. Point and name items, make sounds for animals or vehicles for example.

▫ Put several of baby's favorite toys into a pillow case and give it to her to figure out how to get them out—she will love discovering what's hiding inside!

▫ Putting snacks like puffs or other soft food pieces in egg cartons or ice cube trays continue to work on fine motor skills in getting the pieces out. You can also give baby some puffs in a small cup that he can hold with one hand to work on bilateral skills (coordinating use of both hands),—one hand holds or stabilizes the cup while the other takes out food pieces.

▫ Take time to just be present with baby. Get at baby's level, make eye contact, and see what she initiates. Maybe she hands you a toy. Maybe she crawls up on you for a hug. Maybe she points to something she wants, or reaches toward a favorite item.

▫ Continue lots of sensory play and exploration! Baby may enjoy moving around in ball pits. An idea for a "sensory bin": Fill a large container with cotton balls, and have baby find hidden toys amongst the cotton balls. Sand, mulch and dirt play—close supervision so baby doesn't get sand in eyes or try to eat handfuls! Try playing with potato flakes: try them dry, and try them wet. When mixed with water you can squish and mold into a ball or other things for a taste safe activity. Baby may enjoy poking holes in it.

▫ Bathtub: Fill and dump with cups or other containers, or utensils such as a ladle, or pour water through a strainer. Squeeze squirt toys or sponges. Foam letters and numbers stick to some tub edges and walls when wet. Name body parts you are washing.

▢ Paint with water colors on white paper or "paint" using just water on colored construction paper or outside on a sidewalk.

▢ Crawl and climb over a "mountain" of pillows and cushions or make and obstacle course—crawl through tunnel, then over a pillow, then under a table. Baby may try to push a car along while crawling. Crawl up steps with close supervision.

▢ Mega blocks, hammering toys, and of course bubbles, balls and inflated balloons (supervised). Baby may be enjoying lots of turn taking with rolling a ball back and forth. Say "pop" each time a bubble is popped, and soon baby may imitate.

▢ Play fruit and vegetable halves connected with Velcro are good for little hands—encourage pulling apart to work on hand strength and coordinating using both hands together. You can also adjust to hook together only part of the Velcro so that the halves are easier to pull apart. Duplos or large connecting blocks are great for working both hands to pull apart and can also work on putting together or stacking with help.

▢ Sticky wall and painter's tape activities mentioned in Month 10

▢ Toys with knobs, buttons, cranks, doors or flaps to open, and other items for little fingers to manipulate.

▢ Carrying on a pretend "conversation" using toy phone

▢ When folding laundry, make sock rolls into "balls" your little one can throw into the basket or just practice his throwing skills. He could also stand at the basket and when ready, squat (holding to basket with one hand) to pick up clothing items to help you put in or take out of the basket.

Examples of concerns you may want to talk with your health care provider about,—if your baby:

▢ Has poor head control in an upright position

▢ Needs to use hands to prop in order to maintain a sitting position

▢ Has extreme reactions to touch or when exposed to new textures

- Doesn't enjoy movement play such as being lifted in air or tilted back toward upside-down
- Doesn't show recognition of familiar words
- Doesn't turn when someone calls baby's name
- Does not use fingertips to pick up small food pieces
- Rejects solid foods, preferring only milk
- Doesn't make a variety of sounds
- Doesn't copy sounds, facial expression or simple actions
- Is persistently unable to calm
- Doesn't engage in joyful smiles and back-and-forth interactions with parents/caregivers
- Coughing or choking during feeding or drinking
- Overstuffing mouth with food

NOTES

_____

_____

_____

_____

_____

_____

_____

_____

_____

_____

_____

_____

_____

_____

_____

_____

_____

_____

_____

_____

_____

_____

_____

_____

12

MONTHS

• • •

BABY'S SUPERPOWER

—

Professional Parent Reaction Tester

FINE MOTOR

- ❑ Uses a neat pincer grasp (now easily with the very tip of index finger and thumb) to pick up small food items, with wrist and arm off of surface or table

- ❑ Can hold a container with one hand while placing an object in it with the other hand

- ❑ Places one block on top of another

- ❑ Isolates index finger well to poke and point

- ❑ Grasps a thick crayon with a fisted grasp and may try to imitate a scribble

- ❑ Uses pads of thumb and first 2 fingers to grasp a cylindrical object

- ❑ Turns thick pages of a book and stabilizes/ holds the book with one hand

GROSS MOTOR

- ❑ Takes several steps with hand held

- ❑ May take a few steps independently before losing balance or dropping to floor

- ❑ Stands alone with feet in a wider stance

- ❑ Maintains sitting balance when throwing objects, and when turning body/head to reach objects

- ❑ Creeps up a couple of steps on hands and knees

- ❑ Moves with whole body rhythmically to music

SOCIAL-EMOTIONAL

- ❑ Still prefers to be near parents or caregivers
- ❑ Enjoys imitating people during play
- ❑ Shows preferences for toys and people
- ❑ Explores environment enthusiastically and with curiosity
- ❑ May test parental reactions at bedtime and during feeding, or test responses to his/her behavior
- ❑ Hugs doll or stuffed animal in imitation or when requested
- ❑ Shows fear and hesitation in new situations
- ❑ May have an attachment object—possibly a toy, blanket, or stuffed animal

COMMUNICATION

- ❑ Uses different hand movements or gestures to communicate wants and needs—pointing, reach to pick up, reach and hold hand toward desired object, bang or push at a toy to get repeated effect
- ❑ Shakes head "no"
- ❑ Signals or says "no" to unwanted or disliked food
- ❑ May say a few single words other than "mama" or "dada"
- ❑ Understands tone of voice has meanings
- ❑ Understands several one step requests—"give me the ball", "look at the dog"

❑ Says or tries to say the name of a food he/she wants

❑ Understands "no-no" although may not comply

❑ Jabbers long string of sounds with tone and inflection that sound like conversation

SELF-HELP

❑ Eats many table foods that you do, soft enough if baby doesn't have a lot of teeth yet

❑ Has more experience with chewing food and can move food side-to-side with tongue

❑ Cooperates in undressing by pulling arms/legs out of clothing and anticipates movements

❑ Cooperates in dressing by extending arms and legs

❑ Enjoys bath time and water play

❑ Cooperates in wiping and drying hands

❑ Brings an open cup to mouth with both hands and drinks—may need some assistance

❑ Holds spoon with a fisted overhand grasp and may try to feed self with spilling

❑ Feeding

- **Breast-fed:** Until baby's content 3-5 times/day

- **Bottle-fed:** 6-8 ounces, 2-3 times/day

- **Solid food:** 3 meals, 2 snacks

Talk with your health care provider about recommendations for adding whole milk.

***When introducing a new food, look for signs of a food allergy (rashes, diarrhea, vomiting, irritability, breathing difficulties) while sticking with that food for 3-5 days before introducing a different new food. You may also want to ask your pediatrician for any recommended medications to have on hand in case baby does have an allergic reaction, or other medication needs such as in the case of a fever.

For more information on allergies visit www.foodallergy.org

❑ Sleeps 10-12 hours at night and naps about 2-3 hours during the day split between 2 naps, or may do one longer nap

❑ As mentioned in Month 11 chapter, if baby has been able to successfully manage all previous single textures, he can now move into the soft mechanical textures that are MIXED textures. Because he has mastered the oral motor skills of handling those previous single textures, he should now be able to detect and manage chunks of food within purees or sauces. Besides Stage 3 baby foods with chunks, examples of mixed textures are macaroni and cheese, children's microwaveable meals with food chunks in sauces, spaghetti, lasagna, other casseroles, or cut up pot pie. If he hasn't mastered the soft cubes, and soft mechanical single textures, let him keep practicing until he is ready. In looking ahead, at 13-14 months, baby will be eating many soft table foods in small pieces, and will then move onto harder mechanical foods by 15-18 months—things such as Cheerios and other cereal pieces, saltine crackers, many other crackers, chips, and cookies. It is important to know that baby will continue to increase their oral motor and chewing skills through 24 months, to be able to fully handle a variety of solid textures.

Straw cups and open cups are preferred because sippy cups are used more like bottles in terms of mouth movement. When a child drinks from a sippy cup, you often see front-back jaw movement like you would see when drinking from a bottle. When drinking properly from a straw (where straw is placed only on the lips), you will see up-down jaw movement like we use during sucking.

COGNITIVE AND PLAY

- ❑ Imitates several actions such as pretending to talk on phone

- ❑ Imitates gestures

- ❑ Able to attend to a motivating/interesting activity for up to 10 minutes

- ❑ Can stack some rings on a pole

- ❑ Places cylinder shape into matching hole in container

- ❑ Connects animals with actions and sounds

- ❑ Changes actions through trial and error

- ❑ Curious about everyday objects and how they work—turning knobs, pushing buttons, opening drawers and cupboards

VISUAL

- ❑ Vision is typically as sharp and clear as an adult's
- ❑ Can watch objects that are moving fast
- ❑ Shows sustained visual interest
- ❑ Appears visually oriented at home—understanding where things are in his/her environment
- ❑ Watches an object that he/she throws
- ❑ Watches a ball when rolled back and forth with another

VISUAL-MOTOR

- ❑ Opens a book and turns pages
- ❑ Places an object inside another, such as with a nesting toy
- ❑ Holds palm upward with arm outstretched to reach for object
- ❑ Turns cranks on toys
- ❑ Tries to "catch" a rolled ball and use arms/ hands to roll ball forward toward another
- ❑ May turn over containers to dump out items

SENSORY

- ❑ Hearing is very accurate

- ❑ Enjoys looking and listening at the same time (reading books, or listening to song while watching actions)

- ❑ Loves exploring textures and engaging in messy play

- ❑ Continues to explore things with hands and mouth, close visual inspection and manipulates objects to further investigate sights, sounds, textures.

- ❑ Through exploration, baby continues to learn how to grade speed and pressure of movements such as lifting a cup to get to mouth smoothly.

- ❑ Continues to develop food preferences, but enjoys a greater variety of smells and tastes—may take 10 tries before baby learns to like a new food.

- ❑ Baby's vestibular system (located in the inner ear), vision, and the ability to process information about body position through muscles and joints and sense of touch continue to all coordinate together to help him orient in space, balance, and move efficiently to perform a task at hand.

- ❑ Enjoys a wide variety of music/sounds, touch and movement play

DID YOU KNOW?

By the time your baby is digging into his 1ˢᵗ year birthday cake, her brain has grown to more than double, reaching 60% of adult size.

- As baby is getting more and more mobile (walking or getting close), make sure he cannot push open doors to the outside or to stairs, or reach items he could pull down on himself when standing.

- Avoid leaving the dishwasher open where baby can reach any sharp knives or breakables.

- Even though it's baby's birthday, be cautious to pick up any balloon pieces if a balloon pops as they are a significant choking hazard and make sure baby is always supervised with latex balloons.

What can I do at this age to help support my baby's development?

- You can continue to involve baby in food play—focus is on exploring food in activities when it's not "eating time" but is completely ok if they do eat any of the safe items involved. Examples of food play are:

  - Using food strips to make shapes or funny faces

  - Help baby stack circles of cut zucchini or cut banana

  - Use a celery stick as a "slide" to watch items, such as a Goldfish cracker go "whee!" down the slide

  - Let baby peel a banana or help pull on an orange peel

  - Poke soft items with thin pretzel sticks or use larger pretzel sticks or large thick carrot to "draw" in pudding or yogurt spread out on tray or plate. Baby will also learn how much pressure to apply to items that can break, such as the pretzel stick.

  □ Breaking items or "smashing" them into crumbles with fingers lets baby know how a food item will break apart in their mouth and gives them insight into what that might feel like.

□ Involve baby in clean up—give him a cloth to wipe his tray, his mouth and hands. He may also like to stand up to a cupboard or the fridge with a sponge and imitate wiping and cleaning, as he's learning to help.

□ Your little one may be using several baby signs you've been demonstrating, such as signs for "more", "please", or "all done".

□ Play-Doh play,—of course watching closely if he is wanting to still explore with his mouth a lot! Smash it and poke holes with fingers; push items like pegs into the Play-Doh; roll with a small rolling pin; help him use cookie cutters; place uncooked spaghetti upright poked into the Play-Doh and stack pasta or cereal rings on the spaghetti

□ Push toys and pushing a laundry basket or large box; ride on scoot toys where feet can reach the ground

□ Taste safe sensory bins. *Taste safe* doesn't mean that it will taste good, or that you necessarily want your child to eat a lot of it. But if baby licks it or sneaks some into his mouth, he will be ok. *You of course still always want to supervise an activity like this.* There are many searchable options on the internet, but some examples of taste safe items you can use for sensory exploration in a bin or container are: water, oatmeal, finely ground graham crackers or cereal for "sand", noodles, gelatin, or edible Play Doh. Choose one as the primary item in the sensory bin, and add other items of interest such as washable toy cars, animals, blocks, or cookie cutters.

□ Taste safe paints—use with fingers, a brush or sponges. You will find various recipes and directions when searching these online, such as simply using yogurt and food coloring, or "painting" with condiments, and pudding. Try food pieces such as a broccoli spear as a paint brush or other vegetable and fruit pieces as "stamps".

- Baby may still enjoy colored spaghetti or rice for sensory play, using food coloring. (See recipe in Month 8.) There are many recipes online such as this: https://www.messylittlemonster.com/2017/03/how-to-make-rainbow-spaghetti-sensory-play.html

- You can make ice cubes with food coloring and a Q-tip frozen in each cube. Baby can then hold to the Q-tip, putting the ice cube to paper to paint and create her masterpiece!

- Stuff small pompoms in opening of plastic water/soda bottle to work on fine motor skills and using both hands when holding bottle with one hand while putting pompoms in with other hand.

- Stickers are fun and require a pincher grasp and problem solving how to get the sticker peeled up and how to get it off when stuck to fingers. Fold up part of the sticker to help baby grasp it. Place stickers on each arm for baby to reach across to try to get off.

- Large crayons on paper or try stamping—guiding with regular stamps or use sponges. You can also try stamping activities with pieces of fruit and vegetables.

- Tape a paper towel or toilet paper core to a wall with painter's tape for baby to stand up to and drop pompoms through. He will like to watch them fall and drop to the floor or in a bucket.

- Your little one has probably placed items in slots such as on a toy piggy bank. You can also try fitting playing cards into slots cut into the top of oatmeal container or a box.

- Single piece puzzles with and without knobs; shape sorters; ball drop toys

- All of those B's: Bubbles, blocks, balls and inflated balloons (supervised)—so many options!

- Connecting blocks such as Duplo's or Bristle blocks—great for using both hands to pull them apart.

- Crawling through blanket forts—incorporating flashlight play is fun in a fort, or encourage baby to "catch" the light spot when moved on the floor in a dim room, encouraging crawling and when ready baby can try while walking.

- Singing and songs with actions. Make up songs for different routines—a song when getting dressed, a song he associates with bath time, a song that means it's time to eat, etc. This can help your little one know what's happening and help with learning the beginning and end to activities, such as singing a song indicating it's time to eat and another song or repeated phrase when all done and washing up.

- Continue to provide a language rich environment with talking, reading, telling stories, matching sounds of animals to the animal. Incorporate talking about directions during play—"The car is going *down*", "Airplane goes *up*", "Cow is going *in* the barn", "Your bear is *under* the blanket"

- Dancing and playing with musical toys. You can also make your own! Many things can be used as a drum. Put beans or rice in bottles with secure lids for shakers. Use a paper towel tube for a horn. Babies love to talk and sing through these too!

- Teach hot and cold —label them during times when it's ok for baby to feel something hot or cold such as feel a warm washcloth, something cold from the fridge, or temperature of water. Talk about it feeling hot or cold outside.

- Unwrap "presents" (wrap up some toys in different boxes) or unwrap things in tinfoil. Baby won't mind that it's a familiar toy—it will be more about the surprise of opening!

- Model and imitate pretend play—with a phone, pretend feeding, putting doll or stuffed animal to bed, etc.

- Pull off clothespins attached around edge of a box and place into container

- Community experiences: library story times, play places such as at a mall, playgrounds, parks, zoo or petting zoo, water play at parks, or different museums, farmer's markets, and child friendly local festivals

- If baby is wanting to walk a lot (hands held or maybe independently), try the challenge of walking on different and uneven surfaces outside— grass, dirt, sand, mulch, pebbles, or up/down a ramp. Baby can also walk on different surfaces for a sensory experience—try walking on sticky contact paper on the floor (edges taped to floor with painter's tape) or walking on bubble wrap.

- Simple obstacle courses or "follow the leader"—incorporating crawling or climbing over something or through a tunnel or box. You can have baby take a small ball through an obstacle course to put in a basket at the end.

- Pouring, filling, dumping, and digging outside in dirt, sand or with water play.

- Felt boards—can purchase or make your own. This can be as simple as shapes on the board or having a felt board with items to tell a story.

- Let your little one do as much as possible during dressing. You will see a sense of accomplishment and independence happening. Expand on this with requesting baby to bring you things—"Get your shoes", "Give mommy your socks", or "Get your blanket for nap time".

- Continue to provide choices throughout activities (2 at a time). When possible hold the choices up so baby just can't grab the one he wants, encouraging pointing or using a word/sounds to voice his choice instead.

Examples of concerns you may want to talk with your health care provider about,—if your baby:

- Has limited or fleeting eye contact

- Doesn't babble or imitate sounds

- Doesn't try to imitate or use gestures, or point at objects

- Doesn't attend to pictures in a book

- Does not look toward sounds or respond to his/her name

- Doesn't engage in joyful smiles and back-and-forth interactions with parents/caregivers

- Is coughing or choking during feeding or drinking

- Overstuffs mouth with food

- Is having difficulty with transitioning to softer table foods

- Uses one side of the body significantly more than the other

- Cannot pull to stand or stand when supported

And just like that, your baby is **1**!

Your baby has worked hard at growing, learning and putting a smile on your face as milestones were mastered and memories were made.

Bring on the toddler journey!

NOTES

REFERENCES

American Optometric Association. (n.d.). Infant Vision: Birth to 24 Months of Age. Retrieved May 27, 2020, from https://www.aoa.org/patients-and-public/good-vision-throughout-life/childrens-vision/infant-vision-birth-to-24-months-of-age

Beery, Keith E. and Buktenica, Norman A. et al. (2010). Beery-Buktenica Developmental Test of Visual-Motor Integration, Sixth Edition (BEERY™ VMI 6)

Brain Architecture. (n.d.). Retrieved June 25, 2020, from https://developingchild. harvard.edu/science/key-concepts/brain-architecture/

COUNCIL ON COMMUNICATIONS AND MEDIA. (2016, November 1). Media and Young Minds. Retrieved July 13, 2020, from https://pediatrics.aappublications. org/content/138/5/e20162591

Do Not Use Infant Sleep Positioners Due to the Risk of Suffocation. (2019, April 18). Retrieved August 3, 2020, from https://www.fda.gov/consumers/consumer-updates/do-not-use-infant-sleep-positioners-due-risk-suffocation

Emanuel, M. (n.d.). TummyTime!TM Method. Retrieved May 27, 2020, from https:// www.tummytimemethod.com/tummytimetrade-method.html

Folio, M. Rhonda, and Fewell, Rebecca R. (2002). Peabody Motor Development Chart. Austin, TX; PRO-ED, Inc.

Henderson, N., & American Academy of Pediatric Dentistry. (n.d.). Healthy Smiles—a family guide. Retrieved May 27, 2020, from https://www.aapd.org/assets/1/7/ HealthySmilesGuidebook.pdf

Hill, D. L., & American Academy of Pediatrics. (2016, October 21). Why to Avoid TV for Infants & Toddlers. Retrieved July 13, 2020, from https://www.healthychildren.org/English/family-life/Media/Pages/Why-to-Avoid-TV-Before-Age-2.aspx

Jain, S. (2018, March 22). How Often and How Much Should Your Baby Eat? Retrieved May 27, 2020, from https://www.healthychildren.org/English/ages-stages/baby/feeding-nutrition/Pages/How-Often-and-How-Much-Should-Your-Baby-Eat.aspx

Toomey, Kay A. (2002). *When children won't eat: The SOS Approach to Feeding.* Retrieved from course material and manual September 7, 2008.

Ages & Stages. (n.d.). Retrieved May 27, 2020, from

https://www.healthychildren.org/English/ages-stages/Pages/default.aspx

Where We Stand: Back To Sleep. (2014, July 11). Retrieved May 27, 2020, from https://www.healthychildren.org/English/ages-stages/baby/sleep/Pages/Where-We-Stand-Back-To-Sleep.aspx

Reviewed by Walter, Rhonda S. (2016, June). *Your child's development.* Kidshealth from Nemours https://Kidshealth.org

Best start. (n.d.). *Children's development—Infants* (0-14 months). Retrieved May 26, 2020, from https://beststart.org

Parlakian, Rebecca, and Lerner, Claire. (2016, February 5). *Your baby's development (0-12 months).* Zero to three. Retrieved May 26, 2020, from https://zerotothree.com

Mayo clinic staff. (2017, June 28). *Infant development: Milestones from 0-12 months.* Infant and toddler health. Mayo clinic. Retrieved May 26, 2020, from https://mayoclinic.org

Mayo Clinic Staff. (2017, July 22). Healthy Lifestyle, Infant and toddler health. Pacifiers: Are they good for your baby? Retrieved June 8, 2020, from https://www.mayoclinic.org/healthy-lifestyle/infant-and-toddler-health/in-depth/pacifiers/art-20048140

Mayo clinic staff. (2019, March 7). *Language development: Speech milestones for babies.* Infant and toddler health. Mayo clinic. https://mayoclinic.org

By Lise Eliot, L. (2000). *What's Going on in There? How the Brain and Mind Develop in the First Five Years of Life* . New York, NY: Bantam.

Folio, M., & Fewell, R. (2000). Peabody Developmental Motor Scales—Second Edition (PDMS-2): Peabody Motor Development Chart. Austin, TX: Pro-Ed.

16 Incredibly Cool Facts About Your Baby . (n.d.). Retrieved 29 May 2020, from https://www.pbcexpo.com.au/blog/16-incredibly-cool-facts-about-your-baby

American Academy of Pediatrics. (2018, November 21). Food Allergies in Children. Retrieved June 5, 2020, from https://www.healthychildren.org/English/healthy-living/nutrition/Pages/Food-Allergies-in-Children.aspx

American Academy of Pediatrics. (2019, November 12). Healthy Digital Media Use Habits for Babies, Toddlers & Preschoolers. Retrieved June 29, 2020, from https://healthychildren.org/English/family-life/Media/Pages/Healthy-Digital-Media-Use-Habits-for-Babies-Toddlers-Preschoolers.asp

Greer, F., Sicherer, S., & Burks, A. (2019, April 1). The Effects of Early Nutritional Interventions on the Development of Atopic Disease in Infants and Children: The Role of Maternal Dietary Restriction, Breastfeeding, Hydrolyzed Formulas, and Timing of Introduction of Allergenic Complementary Foods. Retrieved June 5, 2020, from https://pediatrics.aappublications.org/content/143/4/e20190281#xref-ref-30-1

ABOUT THE AUTHOR

Sharon Drewlo, OTR/L, CIMI is a pediatric occupational therapist of more than 30 years and certified infant massage instructor. She is the founder of Forward Therapy Solutions PLLC, offering services for children and families in the home and community as well as through telehealth. Sharon obtained her Occupational Therapy degree from the University of North Dakota in December of 1988. Her professional journey has led her to work in a variety of settings, but it was her work with children and families in their natural environments that she observed children achieving best outcomes in less time, with parents feeling empowered in carrying over recommendations and strategies that supported their child's development and fit into their daily routines.

To contact Sharon or learn more about and Forward Therapy Solutions, please visit:

Website: www.forwardtherapysolutions.com
Email: sdrewlo@forwardtherapysolutions.com

You may also wish to join the private Facebook group—**Purposeful Play in the Everyday**:
www.facebook.com/groups/PurposefulPlayintheEveryday/about

This is a positive and supportive space for all parents and anyone caring for children birth to 5, to learn and share experiences and ideas that promote development through play and in the "everyday"—those activities and daily routines that make your world go round!

Made in United States
North Haven, CT
09 December 2021

12306564R00102